WE WILL REMEMBER THEM

WE WILL REMEMBER THEM

Peter Ridley • Alan Inder • Tony Kippenberger

Published by The Bishop's Waltham Society

Registered Charity Number 1170683

Front cover:
British soldiers go over the top during
the Battle of the Somme 1916

Back cover:
A British soldier stands amongst the ruins of
Ypres 1917

Both with kind permission D&L Educational Supplies

Published by the Bishop's Waltham Society
www.bishopswalthamsociety.org.uk

© Peter Ridley, Alan Inder, Tony Kippenberger 2018

The authors assert their rights under
the Copyright, Design and Patents Act 1988
to be identified as the authors of this work

Designed by Andy Soameson
andyartgecko@gmail.com

Printed by Solent Design Studio Ltd, Claylands Road, Bishop's Waltham

ISBN 978-0-9511449-3-0

CONTENTS

Foreword		6
Preface		8
Chapter 1	An Introduction	11
Chapter 2	The Bishop's Waltham War Memorial	23
Chapter 3	A Background to the Great War 1914-1918	26
Chapter 4	The Men from Bishop's Waltham Who Died in the Great War	32
Chapter 5	A Storyline of the Great War	107
Appendix 1	Where They Lived	131
Appendix 2	Cemeteries and Memorials of the Great War	138
Appendix 3	Medals and Badges	150

POEMS

Socks *Jessie Pope*	10
A Story of Today *Constance Powell*	22
The Soldier *Rupert Brooke*	25
The General *Siegfried Sassoon*	31
Dulce et Decorum Est *Wilfred Owen*	106
In a Soldiers' Hospital: Pluck *Eva Dobell*	130
Warbride *Nina Murdoch*	137
In Flanders Fields *John McCrae*	149
For the Fallen *Laurence Binyon*	156

FOREWORD

I am very proud to write this foreword to an anthology of World War One casualties from Bishop's Waltham and its surrounding villages. It will be read with great interest, not only by the descendants of those who fell, but also by all of today's residents of our mediaeval market town. Peter Ridley, Alan Inder and Tony Kippenberger have, with great dedication and diligence, researched and put together a most interesting collection of human stories of events that took place a century ago but that left an everlasting mark. Even when I was a boy at Curdridge, I have a clear memory of a very dear man who continued to work despite being gassed in what he called the Great War.

A Great War it was, and at the time there was hardly a family in the land that did not know someone or had had a member who fought in the brutal trenches of the Western Front, Gallipoli, in the Royal Navy or the sands of Arabia and Palestine. Two of my uncles perished in the war, one only 19. Even my father-in-law, who was grievously wounded on the Somme, and survived to the ripe old age of 81, never talked about his brief experience, except just one time with me. The family names of many in this book are still living in the communities in and around Bishop's Waltham today. The war had a dramatic effect on the whole nation: 700,000 were killed and memorials such as the Cenotaph on Whitehall in London demonstrate the profound feeling felt by everyone.

Even today as we commemorate the centenary of the end of the conflict, secondary schools all over the country take GCSE History students to tours of the battlefields. As we travel across continental Europe by car or train, the visible evidence of war memorials and cemeteries scattered beside the routes serve as a lasting reminder and prompt enquiring minds.

Peter Ridley has faithfully recorded the last resting place of most of the Bishop's Waltham casualties in various cemeteries in northern France and elsewhere. It is a remarkable piece of research that discovered that one man from Bishop's Waltham also died in the little-known campaign in support of the Italians on the Italian/Austria border, sometimes known as the "White War". In all there are 61 biographies of our Fallen.

It is staggering that the 54,395 names recorded on the Menin Gate in Belgium know no named or marked grave and that memorial does not include those lost in France. Of the six million troops who went to war, 12% of soldiers and 18% of officers did not survive.

By early 1916, the original British Expeditionary Force that had fought the early campaign in Belgium and Picardy had largely disappeared either as casualties or returned to "Blighty". Thus, Lord Kitchener started a huge recruiting drive to establish a "citizen army" to drive the Germans out of France. The new recruits were mostly young, new to battle and most became casualties. One third of that new army never returned home. It is therefore not surprising that most of the Bishop's Waltham's casualties date from that second part of the war.

In 1918 the Germans made one last concerted effort to break through to Paris and beyond. They nearly succeeded but were stopped just short of Amiens by brave resistance of British and Australian troops. Subsequently the Americans entered the fray and fresh troops were able to push the Germans back and so by November, enemy resources were stretched beyond limit and an Armistice was declared at the 11th hour of the 11th day of the 11th month.

Men of Bishop's Waltham took their part in the greatest war the world had known. Peace was restored at great cost and it was a tragedy that the very peace treaty signed at Versailles by all combatant nations, including the Commonwealth dominions for the first time, sowed the seeds for further conflict. As someone once said, the War to end all War was followed by a Peace to end all Peace!

Brigadier David Webb-Carter OBE, MC
Little Ashton Farm, Ashton Lane, Bishop's Waltham

PREFACE

The title of this book, *We Will Remember Them*, refers to those men from Bishop's Waltham who died serving in the Great War. But it is also an opportunity to remember those who lived.

Throughout the war men returned with a "Blighty" – military slang for an injury that was sufficiently serious to merit being shipped home to Britain. With wounds inflicted by shells and shrapnel, bullets and bombs, many would live the rest of their lives disabled by those wounds. As the war dragged on, the increasing use of gas – chlorine, phosgene and then the most dreaded of them all, mustard gas – meant that more men came home crippled, but in different ways.

All the while the fathers, mothers, brothers and sisters of the men, as well as wives and girlfriends, simply had to wait for news of their loved ones. The book gives many of their names. The newspapers carried daily lists of casualties, and people came to dread looking down them lest they recognised a name. Even more feared was the postman delivering a telegram – a small sheet of paper addressed to the next of kin that named the nature and date of death, and a briefly expressed message of sympathy from the War Office. How this repeated process must have felt for the small, close-knit community of Bishop's Waltham it is difficult to imagine.

And even when the war was over and those who survived came back, many if not most carried with them memories of things too awful to describe – images and sounds of what they'd witnessed. Scarred not physically but mentally.

Throughout the book are some war poems chosen to reflect not just those who gave their lives, but also those who lived with the consequences of conflict. We remember them too…

Tony Kippenberger
Chairman
Bishop's Waltham Society

Marguerite Matthews (née Gore) with baby John. She lost her husband William in 1915 and her younger brother in 1917.

Socks

Shining pins that dart and click
In the fireside's sheltered peace
Check the thoughts that cluster thick —
20 plain and then decrease.

He was brave — well, so was I —
Keen and merry, but his lip
Quivered when he said good-bye —
Purl the seam-stitch, purl and slip.

Never used to living rough,
Lots of things he'd got to learn;
Wonder if he's warm enough —
Knit 2, catch 2, knit, turn.

Hark! The paper-boys again!
Wish that shout could be suppressed;
Keeps one always on the strain —
Knit off 9, and slip the rest.

Wonder if he's fighting now,
What he's done an' where he's been;
He'll come out on top somehow —
Slip 1, knit 2, purl 14.

Jessie Pope

Chapter 1

AN INTRODUCTION

"At August Bank Holiday 1914[1] the High Street was thronged with people all discussing one thing: the near certainty of war with Germany if the midnight ultimatum were ignored. The Reservists and the local company of the Hampshire Royal Garrison Artillery had already been called up to man the Sea Defence Stations. The evening wore on and the throng thinned. Midnight came but still no news. Next morning we heard that we were at war with Germany. Patriotism was high and young men in their thousands were clamouring to join the armed forces..."

Bishop's Waltham High Street circa 1910

The purpose of this book is to commemorate the servicemen from Bishop's Waltham who died while serving in the Great War, 1914[1]-1918.

[1] August Bank Holiday fell on Monday 3rd August in 1914, the day before war was declared. Quote taken from *Bishop's Waltham: Parish, Town and Church* by Peter Watkins, from *Parish News* 1972

The original intention back in 2014 was to research and write short biographies of the men whose names are recorded on the War Memorial in the churchyard of St Peter's Church. These would be published in the *Bishop's Waltham & Upham Parish News* in chronological order according to the centenary of the date of their death. While originally focused on the War Memorial, the work also took into account two Rolls of Honour commemorating those who died in the Great War; one is held in Bishop's Waltham Museum and the other is on the wall of St Peter's Church. There are some discrepancies between the lists of men on the War Memorial and in the two Rolls of Honour. Also, some local naval men are commemorated on the Portsmouth Naval War Memorial but not in Bishop's Waltham. It was decided, for the sake of completeness, to include all local servicemen who are listed on the rolls of honour or the Portsmouth memorial even if not on the War Memorial in the churchyard. The complete list is set out in **Table 1** on page 18.

The Roll of Honour in St Peter's Church

INTRODUCTION

Bishop's Waltham in 1911
The population of the Bishop's Waltham area in 1911 (which for census purposes included Upham, Curdridge and Durley) was 4,570. Bishop's Waltham itself had a population of 2,488, so it was a comparatively small town. Nevertheless it had two schools, a gas works, a railway station, a water works, a flour mill, a fire brigade, a technical school, two brick and tile manufacturers, a brewery, nine public houses, five beer retailers, eight solicitors, five butchers, five bakers, two banks, two blacksmiths, and a motor car sales and repair establishment[2]. The essentially agricultural nature of the town at the time was, however, demonstrated by the fact that a great preponderance of the listed commercial operators were farmers or market gardeners. There were also facilities, including public houses and beer retailers, in Upham, Curdridge and Durley.

This is the bustling market town that the men left to go to war.

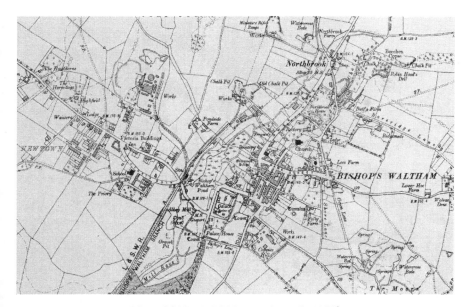

Map of Bishop's Waltham as it was in 1910[2]

[2] Kelly's Directory

Structure

In order to turn this original research into a book, we have broadened its scope to provide a fuller picture of where and how the men died. So the book includes not only the men who died in the Great War but also the story of the War itself.

Chapter 2 tells the story of the War Memorial in St Peter's churchyard.

Chapter 3 provides a background to the Great War – "The war to end all wars".

All the biographies that were the subject of *Parish News* articles – in some cases, amended or expanded – are published in Chapter 4, in alphabetical order of surname. Where we have referred to them elsewhere in the book, we have put their surname in capital letters for ease of reference back to this chapter.

Chapter 5 provides an account of the Great War to explain the different military fronts on which these men fought and to provide a context for the battles and actions in which they laid down their lives.

During the course of this project, work was done to link the servicemen that we have researched to the places in and around Bishop's Waltham where they lived. In many cases their places of residence have disappeared through development, but it is interesting to record a number of dwellings that still exist. This research is summarised in Appendix 1.

In the January 2018 issue of the *Parish News*, an article was published on some of the principal Great War Cemeteries where Bishop's Waltham servicemen are buried and, in cases where their bodies were not found, on Memorials to the missing. Three local servicemen are buried in St Peter's churchyard. This article is reproduced and expanded in Appendix 2.

A wide range of medals and badges were awarded to acknowledge different types of service, and bravery in action. The most relevant to our story are described briefly in Appendix 3.

INTRODUCTION

Sources of Information

The most up-to-date **censuses** that are available for public scrutiny are those for 1891, 1901 and 1911. Most of the young men who went to, but did not return from, the Great War will be listed on at least one, and often on all three, of these documents. They are the real starting point for research.

There are, however, quite a number of others sources. One of the most comprehensive is the **UK Soldiers Who Died in The Great War Index** which gives unit, service number, date and place of death, and lists some 703,000 individuals. There are also **The UK Army Register of Soldiers' Effects,** (this index does not show personal effects, but lists the monetary sums due to next of kin – back pay and war gratuities), **The UK and Commonwealth War Graves** and the **Royal Navy and Royal Marines War Graves Commissions' Sites,** the **British Army WW1 Medal and Award Rolls,** and the **Medal Rolls Index Cards** and, if you can find them, the **British Army and Navy Service Records**. These latter documents are "gold plated" sources, providing lots of information, but as most of the Army records were bombed in WWII it is unusual to be able to find them, and even if they are available, they are generally difficult to decipher due to fire and water damage.

Less important sources include The England & Wales Free Births, Marriages and Deaths Indices (FreeBMD), The National Roll of the Great War, various Unit War Diaries, the England & Wales National Probate Calendar, De Ruvigney's Roll of Honour, Wikipedia, the internet generally, and the many sites devoted to individual regiments or naval ships. New documents are being made available on the internet all the time. More and more Unit War Diaries for WW1 are being added to the records, and recently (although it has no effect on WWI) the 1939 Register has appeared. This is a listing made shortly after the outbreak of WWII, and was intended to provide information for identity cards and ration books. It is not quite a census, but nevertheless, in deference to the 100 year rule, the name and details of any living person on the list is "redacted".

It has to be remembered that genealogy is not an exact science. Amazing coincidences do occur and are known to lead the researcher astray, as does the very human characteristic of quietly altering an unloved forename when completing a census form. The custom that required women to change their surname on marriage can be a snare too. Enumerators' handwriting often leaves a lot to be desired, and the mis-spelling of surnames is a curse. Although a good deal of effort has gone into the avoidance of these pitfalls, there cannot be an absolute guarantee of accuracy.

Note about the Authors

Alan Inder was the instigator of the project and the author of the article on Great War Cemeteries and Memorials (Appendix 2) and the compiler of the table of places of residence in Appendix 1.
He is also the overall editor of this book.

Peter Ridley undertook the very thorough research about the servicemen and is the author of all the biographies Chapter 4.

Tony Kippenberger has provided the background to the Great War in Chapter 3 and researched the different fronts and battles to provide a wider context in Chapter 5.

Acknowledgements

The authors gratefully acknowledge the support and financial assistance of the Bishop's Waltham Society towards publication of this book, and of the producers of the monthly *Bishop's Waltham & Upham Parish News* for publishing some of the material in this book as articles during the period 2014-2018.

We also acknowledge with gratitude the Bishop's Waltham Museum for the use of some of their archive photos; Jurga Van Steenbergen for permission to reproduce photographs of Tyne Cot Cemetery and the Menin Gate Memorial; Rob Day for his photographs of plaques in St Peter's Church; and Tony Kippenberger for additional photographs. We are also very grateful to Carl Graham for his extensive research on the Battle of Jutland. Thanks

INTRODUCTION

also go to Jacky Kippenberger for copy-editing and proof-reading the final version of the book, to Andy Soameson for its design and layout, and to Solent Design for all their help in final print and production.

Several people have contributed information and photographs relating to the servicemen who are commemorated in this book. In particular, we give thanks to the following (the name of the relevant servicemen are in brackets):
Roy King (Francis Higgins)
Geoff May (William Edgar May)
Maggie Jarvis (William Matthews)
Jayne Baylis (Edward/Patrick Gore)
Mike Newberry (Frank Andrews)
Betty Hiscock (Frederick & Thomas Edwin Andrews)
John Osborne (Henry Lacey)
Peter Birkett (Herbert Gibson)

Northbrook House was used as an infirmary for wounded soldiers during the Great War. Here the owners, Mr & Mrs Bamforth, stand outside the front door with some of the nurses.

Table 1: THE MEN WHO DIED

Listed below are the army, naval and air force personnel who are named on the War Memorial in St Peter's Churchyard and/or the Bishop's Waltham Rolls of Honour.

Name	Service	Date of Death	Age	Place of Burial/ Memorial
ANDREWS, Frank	63rd RN Division	April 1918	26	Pozières
ANDREWS, Frederick Charles	Royal Navy HMS *Princess Royal*	31.5.1916	35	Portsmouth Naval Memorial
ANDREWS, Thomas Edwin	Royal Artillery	20.2.1915	20	Bishop's Waltham Churchyard
APPS, John Henry	Canadian Trench Mortar Battery	20.4.1918	34	Wailly Orchard, Pas de Calais
BAILEY, Ralph Ernest	Australian Imperial Forces	27.4.1915	20	Lone Pine Memorial, Turkey
BARFOOT, Edwin Albert	Royal Marines Light Infantry HMS *Queen Mary*	31.5.1916	27	Portsmouth Naval Memorial
BATT, Theophilus	Welsh Regiment	7.11.1918	41	Amara, Iraq
BELL, Charles Albert	Royal Navy HMS *Ghurka*	8.2.1917	30	Portsmouth Naval Memorial
BEST, Ambrose Bert	DoE's Wiltshire Regiment	13.3.1915	34	Le Touret Memorial, Nord Pas de Calais
BRUCE, Donald	King's Royal Rifle Corps	15.5.1915	28	Longueness Cemetery, Nord Pas de Calais
CASEY, George Gordon	Hampshire Royal Garrison Artillery		27	Milton Cemetery, Portsmouth
CONDUCT, Leonard Albert	Hampshire Regiment	6.8.1915	25	Helles Memorial, Turkey
CONDUCT, William Edward	Hampshire Regiment		23	Thiepval, Somme
COOK, Frederick Alexander	Royal Field Artillery		20	Le Touret Military Cemetery, Nord Pas de Calais

INTRODUCTION

COPP, William Jacob	Royal Navy HMS *Glatton*	16.9.1918	21	Portsmouth Naval Memorial
COTTLE, George James	Army Service Corps	20.2.1917	34	Bishop's Waltham Churchyard
CUTLER, William John	Royal Garrison Artillery	5.4.1917	19	Dickebusch New Military Cemetery
DAVIS, Cecil	Royal Warwickshire Regiment	30.8.1918	29	Vis-en-Artois, Nord Pas de Calais
EMMETT, Albert Henry	Gloucestershire Regiment	20.2.1917	28	Pietà, Malta
EMMETT, Alfred Harry	Rifle Brigade	31.7.1915	21	Menin Gate Memorial, Ypres
EPPS, Louis	Hampshire Regiment	1.7.1916	21	Thiepval, Somme
ETHERIDGE, Harry	Royal Navy HMS *Surly*	19.7.1919	36	Bishop's Waltham Churchyard
FURSEY, William Arthur	Royal Garrison Artillery	19.6.1917	21	Lijssenthoek Military Cemetery, Poperinge
GARSIDE, William Henry	Hampshire Regiment		22	Marcoing British Cemetery, Nord Pas de Calais
GIBSON, Herbert	Royal Field Artillery		29	Merville, Nord Pas de Calais
GIBSON, Neil Stewart/Stuart	Hampshire Regiment		24	Baghdad, Iraq
GIFFARD-BRINE, Robin George Bruce	Royal Navy HMS *Invincible*	31.5.1916	17	Portsmouth Naval Memorial
GORE, Edward Patrick	Royal Navy HMS *Tartar*	17.6.1917	16	Portsmouth Naval Memorial
GUNNER, Benjamin George	Northumberland Fusiliers	7.10.1915	23	Brandhoek, Belgium
GUNNER, Edward Geoffrey	Royal Navy HMS *Bulwark*		20	Portsmouth Naval Memorial
GUNNER, John Hugh	Hampshire Regiment	9.8.1918	34	La Clytte, Belgium
HAMMOND, Charlie	Hampshire Regiment	3.9.1916	39	Thiepval, Somme

WE WILL REMEMBER THEM

Name	Regiment/Ship	Date	Age	Memorial/Cemetery
HAMMOND, Herbert	Royal Navy HMS *Partridge*		31	Portsmouth Naval Memorial
HARVELL, Frederick William	Hampshire Regiment	17.4.1917	28	Karasouli, Macedonia, Greece
HEWETT, Howard Dudley	Royal Flying Corps/RAF, 13 Squadron		20	Awoingt British Cemetery, Nord Pas de Calais
HEWETT, William John	Royal Munster Fusiliers	9.5.1915	38	Caberet Rouge Cemetery, Souchez
HIGGINS, Francis	Worcestershire Regiment	27.8.1917	26	Ypres Town Cemetery Extension
KING, Andrew Buchanan	Argyll & Sutherland Highlanders	28.5.1915	40	Hazebrouck, France
LACEY, Henry Percy Walter	Hampshire Regiment	9.8.1916	22	Potijze Chateau Wood, Belgium
LEE, Ernest Edward	Hampshire Regiment	10.4.1917	35	Étaples Military Cemetery, Nord Pas de Calais
LOVELL, George	Royal Navy HMS *Indefatigable*	31.5.1916	36	Portsmouth War Memorial
MATTHEWS, William	Royal Engineers	9.8.1915	30	Menin Gate
MAY, William Edgar	Hampshire Regiment	9.8.1916	21	Potijze Burial Ground Cemetery, Belgium
MEARS, Walter	Royal Navy HMS *Lion*	31.5.1916	29	Portsmouth Naval Memorial
NEWLAND, George William	Rifle Brigade	18.8.1917	25	Tyne Cot, Belgium
PAICE, Archibald Stanley	East Kent Regiment (The Buffs)		36	Hillingdon & Uxbridge Cemetery
PRICE, Jack Benjamin	Royal Horse & Field Artillery	14.7.1917	24	Loos Memorial, Nord Pas de Calais

INTRODUCTION

PRICE, Walter	Hampshire Regiment	26.4.1915	25	Menin Gate, Ypres
PURNELL, Albert Edward	Machine Gun Corps	29.3.1918	20	Pozières, Somme
RICHARDS, Esau	Gloucestershire Regiment		20	Delsaux Farm, Nord Pas de Calais
RICHARDS, George Solomon	Royal Engineers	8.11.1918	39	Gibraltar
RICHARDS, William Henry	Royal Engineers	22.8.1917	23	Étaples, Nord Pas de Calais
SIMS, Arthur Follett	Canadian Infantry	8.10.1916	33	Vimy, Pas de Calais
SIMS, Oswald Follett	Hampshire Regiment	22.1.1917	19	Grove Town Cemetery, Méaulte, Picardy
SMITH, Charles Henry	Dorsetshire Regiment		22	Basra, Iraq
STEELE, William Charles	Hampshire Regiment	29.6.1915	29	Helles Memorial, Turkey
STUBBS, Frank Austin	Royal Fusiliers		28	Terlichtun, Nord Pas de Calais
WATSON, Francis	Highland Light Infantry	4.5.1917	35	Savona, Liguria, Italy
WEAVIL, Reginald Frank	Hampshire Regiment		19	Giavera, Treviso, Italy
WEEKS, Edwin	Gloucestershire Regiment		19	Alexandria
WEEKS, Wilfred Joseph	Devonshire Regiment	2.10.1917	26	Tyne Cot, Belgium

A Story of Today

An open drawer, a woman lowly kneeling,
Some little crimson shoes, a lock of hair,
Some childish toys, an engine and a trumpet,
A headless horse, a battered Teddy bear.
Some school-boy books, all inky, torn and thumb-marked,
A treasured bat, his favourite cricket ball,
The things he loved, the letters that he wrote her –
And now she places on top of all
A soldier's sword, his photograph, in khaki –
The boyish eyes smile back into her eyes,
While in her hand she holds a V.C. tightly,
And in her heart a grave in Flanders lies.

Constance Powell

Chapter 2

THE BISHOP'S WALTHAM WAR MEMORIAL

The War Memorial at Bishop's Waltham is of plain stone, and takes the form of a cross on a tapering column with a plinth and base. It is located in the corner of the churchyard closest to St Peter's Street, and initially displayed the names of casualties of The Great War only, although in later years the names of the dead of World War II and The Falklands War were added.

The Hampshire Archives have some records relating to our War Memorial. These include the Committee Minutes from the planning meetings, and a copy of the printed programme for the Dedication Service. The minutes are sparse and difficult to read but do show that both Admiral George Augustus Giffard and Charles Richards Gunner (both of whom lost sons) were notable members of the Committee.

The first meeting was held on 5th February 1919 and the last on 23rd April 1923. No indication is given as to how the list of names to be inscribed on the memorial was drawn up, but discussions did take place about location, with some favouring The Square and others the churchyard. In the event the churchyard was the preferred site, and the Committee appointed Stanley Vaughan as the architect, and Garrett & Hayson as the masons, to design and construct the Memorial. It was dedicated on 3rd August 1921 by the Right Reverend Lord Bishop of Southampton.

Interestingly, on the outside cover of the printed programme for the Dedication Service, handwritten in pencil, are the following names: "Frank Anderson, Bruce, Copp, Gore, Garside, Matthews", and in ink "Best, Ambrose Bert", and again in pencil "names to be engraved on stone memorial". On the inside of the programme, once more in pencil, "Phillip" is scored out and "Jack" added in relation to "Price", while the name "W. H. Garside" is added. It seems likely that these alterations were made by one or other of the Committee members, either at or soon after the dedication, and before the war memorial papers were handed over to Hampshire Archives.

THEY DIED THAT WE MIGHT LIVE

The Soldier

If I should die, think only this of me:
That there's some corner of a foreign field
That is for ever England. There shall be
In that rich earth a richer dust concealed;
A dust whom England bore, shaped, made aware,
Gave, once, her flowers to love, her ways to roam,
A body of England's, breathing English air,
Washed by the rivers, blest by the suns of home.

Rupert Brooke

Chapter 3

A BACKGROUND TO THE GREAT WAR 1914-1918

The Causes of War
Although the trigger for the outbreak of war was the assassination of Archduke Franz Ferdinand of Austria by a Bosnian-Serb in Sarajevo on 28th June 1914, the causes of war were much wider and deeper. Since the 1890s, under Kaiser Wilhelm II, Germany had moved to a more aggressive stance. This had resulted in re-alignments between the European states as well as an arms race on land and sea. By 1914 Europe was divided into two power blocks: Germany, the Austro-Hungarian Empire and Italy (the Triple Alliance, also known as the 'Central Powers') and France, Russia and Britain (the Triple Entente, later known more commonly as 'the Allies').

Britain's involvement
It is a little recognised fact that between the Battle of Waterloo in June 1815 and the Battle of Mons in August 1914, no British soldier had died in action in continental Europe – very nearly 100 years. During this period Britain had remained detached from the constant wars and revolutions that had convulsed Europe for most of the 19th century. However, in 1898, Germany had begun to build up its navy. Recognising a significant threat to her security, Britain abandoned the policy of staying aloof from entanglements with the continental powers and concluded treaties with two of her previous rivals, France (in 1904) and Russia (in 1907).

The opening days
After the assassination in Sarajevo, Germany swiftly offered its unconditional support to Austria-Hungary if it decided to attack Serbia. Austria-Hungary duly declared war on Serbia on 28th July 1914. This was followed by a string of army mobilisations and declarations of war across Europe, and by 1st August Germany had declared war on Russia. On 3rd August Italy declared its neutrality (thus breaking the Triple Alliance) while Germany declared war

on France. The following day German troops invaded Belgium and Britain declared war on Germany. The British Expeditionary Force (BEF) started to land in France four days later on 7th August 1914.

On the 5th August Field Marshal Lord Kitchener was made Secretary of State for War and the next day asked Parliament for permission to expand the army. His appeal to raise this New Army was splashed across the press on the following morning. He set out to raise 100,000 volunteers and asked for men aged between 19 and 30, 5 foot 3 inches or more tall with a chest size greater than 34 inches who would sign up for the duration of the war. There was a huge response across the country and his recruiting poster remains recognisable today.

Lord Kitchener's recruitment poster 1914

War goes global
However this was not going to be just a war on the European continent. In all, over 30 nations declared war between 1914 and 1918. Britain and France were major colonial powers with interests around the world, Germany and Belgium had colonies in Africa. So fighting would involve conflicts around the globe between many different forces, on a geographical scale never before

seen. Fighting occurred not only on the Western Front, but in eastern and south-east Europe, the Middle East and Africa, and soldiers from many countries fought alongside each other – Japan, one of the Allies, sent Japanese warships around the world to help the Royal Navy patrol the Mediterranean.

Industrial warfare in the trenches

The Great War was an unexpected introduction to a new form of warfare. In the early weeks of the war seven Imperial German armies swept through much of Belgium, Luxembourg and north-east France. However it quickly became a war of attrition, as both sides became deeply entrenched along the 440 miles of trenches and fieldworks that stretched from the Belgian coast to the Swiss border. In the main, the British army occupied the part of the line that stretched from Ypres in Belgium down to the river Somme at Amiens in France.

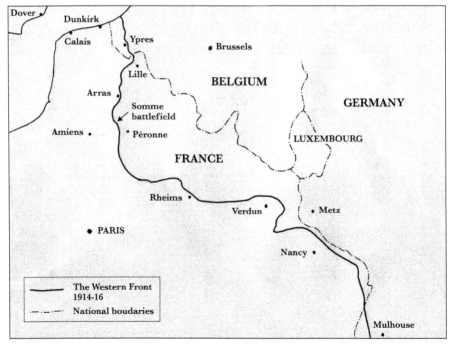

The map shows the 440 mile long Western Front

This static form of warfare was new to all participants and it led to very costly attempts to break out and take ground from the opposite side. Heavy artillery bombardments, exposed advances on foot across 'no man's land' and hand-to-hand fighting in the trenches, became the pattern for set battles. But, apart from such set pieces, probes by both day and night, constant sniper attacks and repeated shelling were all part of the daily routine for those on the front line. Fighting units moved from a period of rest and training to the 'reserve' trenches before being moved up to the front line. After a period in the forward trenches they would once again be relieved and moved back for rest and recuperation. Conditions in the trenches were often appalling.

This type of warfare became a repeated feature on many of the fronts that developed during the war. For example on the Eastern front (with Russia), the Salonika front (against Bulgaria) and at Gallipoli (against Turkey). It was hugely costly in terms of casualties.

Industrialisation and the railways meant that not only could thousands of troops be moved rapidly from one theatre of war to another, but the material of war could be constantly replenished from highly productive factories many miles behind the lines. The scale of production to fight the war was extraordinary. By 1918 Britain alone had produced 4 million rifles, 250,000 machine guns, 52,000 aeroplanes, 2,800 tanks, 25,000 artillery pieces and over 170 million rounds of artillery shells[1].

Technological improvements also meant that new and deadlier weapons were constantly being introduced – from advanced aircraft design to the development of the tank. By 1918, the Germans had developed a gun that could fire shells weighing nearly 250 lbs over a distance of 75 miles – enabling them to shell Paris from behind their lines.

At sea and in the air
The war at sea meant that the two most powerful navies in the world faced each other, although there was only one full confrontation – at the Battle

---

[1] Imperial War Museum

of Jutland. But the contest between the surface vessels and submarines or U-boats, and the danger of underwater minefields took a weekly toll of ships and their crews.

In the air, the arrival of the aircraft as a weapon of war would introduce aerial combat (or dogfights) and then its use as a means to accurately drop bombs on ground troops and strafe them from above.

And in the end…
By mid-1918 not only were the first American troops making their presence felt as the might of the US war machine got into gear but the German economy, blockaded for four years by the British Navy, began to collapse and supplies for the front line troops became short.

Through September and October 1918 the Allies broke through the Hindenburg Line in France and in a succession of battles pushed back the German army. By early November the Imperial German Army was defeated and an Armistice on the Western Front was agreed for 11.00 o'clock on 11 November. The guns finally fell silent and four years of warfare came to an end.

Over 65 million men had volunteered or been conscripted to fight in mass citizen armies. Casualties were horrendous. It is estimated that the total number of military and civilian casualties was more than 41 million (18 million killed and 23 million wounded). Of those killed, around 10 million were military personnel killed in action, two million died of disease and six million were recorded 'missing presumed dead'.

This is the war in which these men from Bishop's Waltham laid down their lives.

The General

"Good-morning; good-morning!" the General said
When we met him last week on our way to the line.
Now the soldiers he smiled at are most of 'em dead,
And we're cursing his staff for incompetent swine.
"He's a cheery old card," grunted Harry to Jack
As they slogged up to Arras with rifle and pack.

But he did for them both by his plan of attack.

Siegried Sassoon

Chapter 4

THE SERVICEMEN FROM BISHOP'S WALTHAM WHO DIED IN THE GREAT WAR

These are the men whose names are recorded on the Memorial in the churchyard of St Peter's Church and in the Rolls of Honour. Their brief biographies were originally published over a period of four years in the *Bishop's Waltham & Upham Parish News*. Many of them belonged to large local families and were related by kinship and marriage.

THE ANDREWS BROTHERS
The family
The 1901 Census shows Frederick Andrews as head of family, aged 46 (a carter on a farm), living at the Franklin Farmhouse, Corhampton, with his wife Jane Andrews (née Sharp) aged 45, and their seven children: Eliza aged 22, Frederick 20, John 19, Burtie 15, William 12, Frank 9, and Edwin 7. Also at the same address are Walter aged 1 (grandson), and John Sharpe 79 (father-in-law). Curiously Edwin's place of birth is given as "Sussex, New England".

By 1911, when the next census was taken, changes had taken place. Eliza, John, William, and Frank had flown the nest but confirmation is given that Frederick senior and Jane had been married for 33 years, and that seven children had been born to them, all of whom were then still alive. The family address was The Avenue, Newtown, Bishop's Waltham. Sometime between 1911 and 1915, Frederick and Jane moved to Beeches Hill.

THE SERVICEMEN FROM BISHOP'S WALTHAM WHO DIED IN THE GREAT WAR

The Avenue, where the Andrews family lived, in 1909

Frederick Charles ANDREWS (1881-1916)
From shepherd to Royal Marine gunner

Frederick, their eldest son, was born in Durley in 1881. He worked as a shepherd and farm labourer until he joined the Royal Marines Artillery as Gunner No.10303. He was killed, aged 35, on 31st May 1916 at the Battle of Jutland, when HMS *Princess Royal*, a 27,000-ton Lion Class battle cruiser with a crew of almost a thousand, was hit nine times by German shells. Some 20 men were killed and 80 injured as a result. The *Princess Royal* was credited with five hits on German vessels, and her own damages were repaired within about six weeks.

Frank ANDREWS (1892-1918)
A Royal Marine for nine years

Their sixth child, Frank, was born in 1892, the event being registered at Midhurst, Sussex. By 1911 he had moved out of the family house in Corhampton and was in the Royal Marines Light Infantry barracks at Alverstoke, having joined the Marines in 1909, with the Service Number of

15544. Frank married Maude Houghton in 1914. Their family home was at 4 Victoria Buildings, Bishop's Waltham, and they had two daughters, Maude junior, and Kathleen Phyllis.

In 1916 Frank was drafted to Mesopotamia in modern-day Iraq, where he took part in engagements at Kut and Baghdad. Later that year he was sent to France, attached to the 63rd Royal Naval Division. He saw service at Cambrai and the Somme, where he was wounded. In April 1918 he was killed in action near Ancre, aged 26. He is commemorated at the Pozières military cemetery.

4 Victoria Buildings, where Frank Andrews' family lived, is in the centre behind the children

(Thomas) Edwin ANDREWS (1894-1915)
A gunner in the Royal Artillery

The 1901 Census shows that their youngest brother, Edwin Andrews, aged 7, was born in 1894. However the 1911 Census lists him as Thomas Andrews, then aged 17. Other records (notably the UK Soldiers Died in the Great War and the England & Wales Free Births, Marriages and Deaths Index) list a Thomas Edwin Andrews, and these and the age and family continuities between the two censuses suggest strongly that Edwin and Thomas were in fact one and the same person – he probably just preferred Thomas over Edwin. He enlisted in the Royal Artillery at Portsmouth as Gunner No.1995, and died in February 1915 of a pneumothorax (collapsed lung), having become ill while under training at Bordon Camp. He was 20. He is buried beneath a military headstone in St Peter's Churchyard, Bishop's Waltham.

Frederick Andrews senior died in 1914, and so was spared the knowledge of the wartime deaths of three of his six sons.

> In Affectionate Remembrance of
>
> ## Thomas Edwin,
>
> The beloved Son of William Fredrick and Jane Andrews of Bishops Waltham
>
> Who departed this life February 20th, 1915,
>
> Aged 20 Years,
>
> And was interred at Bishops Waltham Churchyard.
>
> Beeches Hill
> Bishops Waltham   With the family's kind regards.

Memorial card for Thomas Edwin Andrews

John Henry APPS, M.M. (1884-1918)
Won the Military Medal

John was born in 1884 in Bishop's Waltham to George Henry Apps and Louisa Helen Apps (née Child), the first of their 14 children. The 1891 Census shows him, aged 7, living with his parents and two sisters at Northbrook, Bishop's Waltham, next door to his grandparents, George and Elizabeth

Apps. George senior was a builder and County Court High Bailiff. In the 1901 Census for Bishop's Waltham, although the Apps families were still living at Northbrook, John was missing, but found, now a 17 year old railway clerk lodging with the Gamblin family at 98 Gladstone Road, Bournemouth. Examination of the 1911 British Census ten years later shows no sign of John, but he does appear in the Canadian Census for that year, living in New Westminster, British Columbia, having apparently emigrated in 1907.

Northbrook where John Apps' mother lived – circa 1910

A Canadian attestation form records that John joined the 29th Battalion of the Canadian Overseas Expeditionary Force, as Private No.75454, in November 1914. At that time he was described as being 30 years and 8 months of age, 5' 10" in height, of fair complexion, and having dark brown eyes and hair. He sailed from Montreal to England on board the SS *Missanabie* on 20th May 1915, and seems to have been transferred to France on 24th March 1916.

The next relevant document (a citation card) shows that by April 1917 John had joined the 6th Canadian Trench Mortar Battery, a specialist unit fighting on the Western Front. The card records that he was awarded the Military Medal, "for conspicuous bravery and devotion to duty on April 9th 1917, near THELUS. After the objective had been reached he showed exceptional bravery in getting the guns into position under a very heavy enemy bombardment. On April 10th the battery had orders to take four guns into STATION WOOD just east of FARUS. Pte. Apps was in charge of one, firing 40 rounds with great effect. His example on this occasion greatly inspired his crew under most trying conditions and heavy hostile shelling." (The capital letters used for place names in the foregoing paragraph are exactly as they appear in the citation.)

A year later on 20th April 1918, John, by then a corporal, was killed in action in the Wailly area, near Arras. He was 34 and is buried in the Wailly Orchard Cemetery. The Canadian Grave Registry Form shows his next of kin as Mrs Louise Helen Apps, Northbrook, Bishop's Waltham, near Southampton, England.

Ralph Ernest BAILEY (1895-1915)
A soldier in the Australian Imperial Forces

Ralph was born in Bishop's Waltham in 1895. The 1901 Census shows him living at Mayles Farm, Wickham, with his father Walter Cleveland Bailey, his mother Susannah, and his two brothers Walter and Arthur. By 1911 the family had moved to Green Lane Farm, Bishop's Waltham, and a daughter, Grace, had been born. The Census reveals that the Baileys had then been married for 20 years, during which time five children had been born, of whom four were still living. Unusually both parents had been born in the USA, his father Walter is recorded as being born in Ohio of British parents, and his mother Susannah (née Beck) in New York. It is interesting to note that the 1881 Census shows Susannah living with her parents in High Street, Bishop's Waltham – her father George apparently kept a tailor's shop.

Several family trees and various travel records indicate that between 1911 and 1914, all three Bailey brothers immigrated to Australia and settled in Yanco, New South Wales. Ralph, the youngest, enlisted in the 4th Battalion of the Australian Imperial Forces as Private No.248, on 27th August 1914. His attestation form describes him as aged 22, 6'2" in height, weighing 12st 4lbs, of fair complexion, with grey eyes and (surprisingly) light grey hair. He embarked from Sydney for Europe on the troopship SS *Euripides* on 20th October 1914, and subsequently took part in the landing at Gallipoli on 25th April 1915. He was badly wounded during the operation, evacuated to the hospital ship, SS *Huntsen*, and died two days later on 27th April 1915, aged 20. He was buried at sea, in the Dardanelles. Besides being named on the Bishop's Waltham War Memorial, Ralph is commemorated at the Lone Pine Memorial in Turkey, and at the ANZAC Memorial Clock in Leeton, NSW.

His brothers, Walter and Arthur, remained in Australia, the former dying in 1973 aged 80, and the latter in 1981 aged 87. Both married and had children. His sister Grace stayed in England. She did not marry and died in Portsmouth, aged 74.

It has not been possible to trace the fifth child of Walter and Susannah. It is likely that he or she was born and died between censuses.

The *Huntsend* was originally SMS *Lutzow*, a German passenger liner launched in 1907 of some 8,800 tons, which had been captured in the Suez Canal in August 1914. She was renamed *"Huntsend"* but reverted to *"Lutzow"* when she was sold back to the Norddeutscher Lloyd company in 1923.

Edwin Albert BARFOOT (1889-1916)
On board HMS Queen Mary at Jutland

Edwin was born on 20th October 1889 in Bishop's Waltham, the seventh son of Edward Barfoot, a labourer in the brickworks, and Emma Jane Barfoot (née Varndell). In 1901 he was living with his parents and siblings at 2 Claylands Cottages, Bishop's Waltham. Ten years later the 1911 Census shows that the family had moved to 8 Victoria Road, but by then Edwin had already joined the Royal Marines and was living in barracks in Gosport.

He actually enlisted in the Royal Marines Light Infantry, Portsmouth

Division, as Private No.14966, on 5th September 1907. He was killed in action on 31st May 1916, aged 26, at the Battle of Jutland, when HMS *Queen Mary* (a Lion Class battle cruiser of about 27,000 tons) was sunk with the loss of 1,266 officers and men. Only 20 of the crew survived, 18 being rescued by British destroyers and two by German vessels.

The official history reports that the *Queen Mary* had become the target of both SMS *Derfflinger* and SMS *Seydlitz*, "when at 4.26 a plunging salvo crashed upon her deck forward. In a moment there was a dazzling flash of red flame where the salvo fell, and then a much heavier explosion rent her amidships. Her bows plunged down, and as the *Tiger* and *New Zealand* raced by her to port and starboard, her propellers were still slowly revolving high in the air. In another moment, her two consorts were smothered in a shower of black debris, and there was nothing left of her but a dark pillar of smoke..."

Edwin is commemorated on the Portsmouth Naval Memorial. His body was not recovered for burial, but the wreck of the *Queen Mary* was found in1991 and the site is protected against disturbance by the Protection of Military Remains Act, 1986.

Victoria Road, where the Barfoot family lived at the top of the hill, in 1909

Theophilus BATT (1877-1918)
A baker and insurance agent who died in the desert

James Batt and Rosa Batt (née Lucas) were both born in 1846, James in Bishop's Waltham, and Rosa in Curdridge. They married in 1877 and their first child, Theophilus, was born towards the end of that year. It is difficult to understand what impelled them to choose such an unusual name for their son – the word is Greek and means "beloved of God". Impressive it may be, but it was probably a burden to him at school! Certainly when he filled in his own census form in 1911 he entered himself as "Theo Batt".

Theophilus grew up with his parents and siblings in Bank Street, where his father operated an unusual combination of trades, as a grocer and tailor. He stayed in the family house until 1901, when he married Rosetta Reeves, a Bishopstoke girl. The 1911 Census shows Theophilus, a baker and confectioner, living at 1 Park Road, Bishop's Waltham, with his wife Rosetta and their daughter, Frieda Constance, then aged 7. He seems to have had another string to his bow, as Kelly's Directory for 1911 records him as an insurance agent.

Park Road, where Theo Batt and his family lived, circa 1910

Theo Batt joined the Army, probably in1915, at Southampton, initially as Private No.04816 in the Royal Army Ordnance Corps, being subsequently transferred as Private No.58931 to the 8th (Service) Battalion (Pioneers) of the Welsh Regiment. He died on 7th November 1918 in Mesopotamia, and is buried in the Amara War Cemetery, Al 'Amarah, Iraq. At 41, he was older than most of his comrades. His effects were sent to his widow and daughter.

There were many casualties from illness during the Mesopotamian campaign – typhoid and cholera were rife. As Theophilus is described as having died, rather being killed in action, it is likely that he succumbed to disease.

Charles Albert BELL (1886-1917)
A stoker on HMS *Ghurka*

Charles Albert Bell was born on 4th May 1886 in Micheldever to Charles and Jane Bell. Charles senior died in 1888 and Jane was left to bring up the family by herself, which can't have been easy. The 1901 Census records her living in Bank Street, Bishop's Waltham "on her own means" with her daughter Rachel (26) and sons, James (23) who working as a navvy on the railway, and Charles (14), a labourer in the brickyard. The 1911 Census shows Jane, by then 67, living by herself at Bank Street, all eight of her surviving children having left home. She died in 1932.

Charles signed on for 12 years in the Royal Navy on 7th March 1905. His Service Number was 308296. At the time he was described as being 5' 7" tall, and having light brown hair, grey eyes and a fair complexion. In 1911 the Census records him (aged 24) as one of the crew of HMS *Speedwell* (a Sharpshooter Class torpedo gunboat) then moored at Sidmouth in Devon. In August 1914 he joined HMS *Ghurka* as a Stoker 1st Class. This vessel was a Tribal Class destroyer, built by Hawthorn Leslie & Co., and launched in 1907. At the outbreak of war she joined the 6th Destroyer Flotilla (the Dover Patrol) and was involved in the destruction of the U-8. The spelling 'Ghurka', instead of the more usual 'Gurkha', was in fact used in the naming of this ship.

Ghurka hit a mine off Dungeness on 8th February 1917, and sank with the loss of 74 of her crew of 79, among them Charles, then aged 30. He is commemorated on the Portsmouth Naval Memorial.

Bank Street, where Charles Bell and his mother lived

Ambrose Bert BEST (1880-1915)
Received the 1914 Star and Clasp

John Best married Jane Martin at Iwerne Minister, Dorset, on 9th November 1874. They had 14 children, of whom ten were still living in 1911. Ambrose himself was born in Wimborne, Dorset, in 1880. He was entered as 'Ambrose Berty' on his baptismal record, his paternal grandfather being called Ambrose. The 1891 Census shows him, aged 10, living with his parents and siblings at Bishopstone, Wiltshire. Ten years later, Ambrose is working away from the family as a carter at Ruddlesmon Farm, West Tisbury, Wiltshire, but by 1911 he had returned to the family home, now at 1 Clayland Road, Bishop's Waltham, and was living there, with his parents and two of his brothers.

There is a record in the Royal Navy Register of Seamen's Services showing that an Ambrose Best, who was born in Dorset on 11th September 1880, joined the Navy for a 12 year engagement on 12th April 1899, but was invalided out after about two months, on 9th June 1899. This may have been "our" Ambrose making an early attempt to join the Forces.

Ambrose enlisted at Eastleigh, probably at the outset of war, as Private No.6139, in the 2nd Battalion of the Duke of Edinburgh's Wiltshire Regiment, and arrived in France on 20th October 1914. He was killed in action between 10th and 13th March 1915, aged 34, at the Battle of Neuve Chapelle, and is entitled to the 1914 Star and Clasp, in addition to the usual Service and Victory medals. His name is inscribed on the Le Touret Memorial, Richebourg-l'Avoue, Nord-Pas-de-Calais, France. His effects were sent to his father, John Best, but he died in 1918 and Ambrose's War Gratuity was then sent to his mother, Jane, in 1919.

Donald BRUCE (1887-1915)
A brewer's son killed at Ypres
Donald Bruce joined the 3rd battalion of the Kings Royal Rifle Corps as Rifleman No.7682 at Ealing in 1914. He died of wounds, aged 28, on 15th May 1915 at St Omer, and is buried at the Longuenesse Cemetery in the Pas de Calais. No specific information seems to be available as to the circumstances of his death, but it is known that the 3rd Battalion was involved in the second battle of Ypres, which took place at about this time.

His parents, Francis Robert Bruce and Ellen Mary Bruce (née Dickinson), had married in Kingston-upon-Thames in 1874 and at the time of the 1881 Census were living there, at Richmond Road, with one daughter and two sons. Francis is described then as a "brewer and manager". By 1891 the family had moved to a house called St Margarets, Framfield Road, Uckfield. Francis had advanced to "aerated water maker and bottled beer merchant" by this time, and they had six children, the youngest of whom was Donald, then 4 years old, having been born in about 1887. The house at Uckfield remained the family home until after 1901, but at some time before 1909, when Ellen Mary died, Donald's parents moved to Bishop's Waltham to run a small market garden. The 1911 Census shows Francis Robert (58) living alone in Dean. It seems likely that Francis later moved to Charlton Adam, in Somerset, probably to be near one of his married daughters, and died in 1941.

George Gordon CASEY (1887-1914)
A territorial gunner who died of a cerebral abscess

George joined the territorial army on 13th April 1910 when he was 23, signing on initially for four years as Gunner No.656 in the Hampshire Royal Garrison Artillery. In April 1914 he re-engaged for a further four years, and so was already in the Army when WWI began. He was assigned to serve on the Spit Bank Fort, part of the Portsmouth sea defences. He became ill in November 1914, and was admitted to the Alexandra Hospital, Cosham, on the 18th suffering from a cerebral abscess. He died on 29th November 1914, aged 27. This is borne out by a letter from his mother to her MP, John Hodge, enquiring about a pension, and which forms part of George's Army records. It says, "he went with his company to Spit Bank Fort, from which he went to hospital in Portsmouth, where he died on November 29th 1914 ... after an operation for Polypus". The Find a Grave Index reports that George is buried at the Milton Cemetery, Portsmouth.

George's Army records state that in 1910 he was a schoolmaster by profession, was employed by the Hampshire County Council, and was living in Bishop's Waltham. Kelly's Directory for 1911 names him as Assistant Master at the Bishop's Waltham Boys School (whose Headmaster was Ebenezer Sims – see under entry for SIMS). Although George was certainly with his parents in Portsmouth on the day of the 1911 Census, it seems entirely possible that he had lodgings in BW during the week and returned to his parents at holiday times and weekends.

George had been born in about 1887, the first child of Patrick Albert Casey and Alice Casey (née Gallery). His parents went on to have two more children, Victor Harold (born in 1889) and another, name and sex unknown (born and died between 1901 and 1911). His father was a career seaman in the Royal Navy, who spent much time at sea and was one of the crew of the Royal Yacht, HMS *Ophir*, which carried the Duke and Duchess of Cornwall and York (later to become King George V and Queen Mary) on a tour of the British Empire, which lasted from February to November 1901.

George left a Will, with probate being granted at Winchester, which confirms his death on 29th November 1914 at the "Eye and Ear Hospital at Portsmouth". It shows that he left £263.2s.2d. to his mother, "Alice Casey (wife of Patrick Albert Casey)".

Victor, George's younger brother, was an engineer who apparently became a merchant seaman. He survived the War and became a sugar factory manager in India.

Leonard Albert CONDUCT (1890-1915)
A casualty at Gallipoli
Private No.9482, Leonard Albert Conduct, was killed in action on 6th August 1915, aged 25, at Gallipoli, while serving with the 2nd Battalion of the Hampshire Regiment. He was entitled to the 1914-15 Star in addition to the usual War and Victory Medals. Leonard is named on the Helles War Memorial at Gallipoli but his burial place is unknown. The 2nd Battalion landed in the Cape Helles area on 25th April 1915, and suffered heavy casualties from both military action and disease while fighting near the village of Krithia, before being withdrawn to Egypt in 1916.

Leonard was born in Bishop's Waltham in 1890, the second son of Samuel and Beatrice Conduct (née Smith). At the time of the 1911 Census, Samuel, a fishmonger, and Beatrice had been married for 23 years, and were living at 15 Victoria Buildings, Bishop's Waltham, with their eight children, including Leonard, who at that time was working as a general labourer at the Brick and Tile Works. His younger brother, William Edward, who was killed on the Somme some 18 months later in 1916 (see below), was also living in the family house and working for the same employer.

William Edward CONDUCT (1893-1916)
Local brick maker killed on the Somme

William Conduct was born in Bishop's Waltham in the latter part of 1893. The 1911 Census shows him, aged 19, living with the family at 15 Victoria Buildings, and working with Leonard, his elder brother, in the Brick and Tile Works. Probably towards the end of 1914, William joined the 2nd Battalion of the Hampshire Regiment as Private No.14650. He was sent to France on 25th April 1915 and was killed in action on 13th October 1916. He was 23. He is listed at the Thiepval Memorial Cemetery, Picardie, France.

The Battalion's War Diary reports that after a general attack on 12th October the Hampshires were sent in to consolidate the position in a newly captured trench. During the next day they were fired upon with rifle grenades from an enemy position to their left, but "replied with good effect, although 12 of our men were killed, and 44 wounded". It seems likely that William was killed in this action. In addition to the Service and Victory medals, William was entitled to the 1915 Star. His effects were sent to his father, Samuel.

William's elder brother, Leonard, had been killed in action the previous year.

Frederick Alexander COOK (1897-1916)
Twice mentioned in despatches

Frederick Alexander Cook was born in 1897 in Wickham, the first child of Frederick William Cook and Rosetta Cook (née Alexander). His second forename was probably given in honour of his maternal grandfather, Edward Alexander, a barge builder of Reading, Berkshire.

In 1901 Frederick senior was working as a coachman and the family was living at 11 Claylands Cottages. Frederick Alexander was by then 4 years old and had two younger brothers, Charles and Arthur. Ten years later the census records their address as 1 Pondside Terrace, Bishop's Waltham, and Frederick William's occupation as gardener, while Frederick Alexander, then 14, is shown as a gardener's boy – presumably helping his father.

In August 1914 Frederick Alexander volunteered for the Royal Field Artillery as Private No.87427, and was sent to France in July 1915 with the "Y" 5th Trench Mortar Battery. He fought at the battles of Ypres, Delville Wood and the Somme, was twice mentioned in despatches, and promoted to corporal. On 26th December 1916 he was killed in action, aged 20. He is buried at the Le Touret Military Cemetery, Richebourg-l'Avoué. In addition to the General Service and Victory medals, he was entitled to the 1914-15 Star.

William Jacob COPP (1897-1918)
Career Navy Man died in the HMS *Glatton* Explosion

William Jacob Copp was born in Lymington on 5th November 1897, son of William Copp and Annie Copp (née Davis). The 1901 Census shows him living with his parents and sisters (Honor and Queenie) at Pitts Deep Coastguard Station, Boldre. By 1911 the family had moved to Hangers Hill, Bishop's Waltham, but by then William Jacob had already left home.

William enlisted in the Royal Navy at Portsmouth as a Boy (Service Number J/10584) in December 1910, and probably deliberately mis-stated his age in order to join earlier than the regulations allowed. He subsequently undertook a 12 year engagement, starting on 5th November 1912 (his 15th birthday), at which time he was described as being 18 years old, 5'7" tall, with brown hair, blue eyes and a fresh complexion.

By 1918 he had progressed from Boy, through the ranks of Ordinary Seaman, Able Seaman and Leading Seaman, to Petty Officer. In the second quarter of 1918 William married Jessie Howick, an Emsworth girl. Their union was registered at Havant.

Most of his wartime service was on board HMS *Inconstant*, a 3,500-ton light cruiser, which took part in and survived the Battle of Jutland. However, on 31st August 1918 he was appointed to HMS *Glatton*, a 5,800-ton Gorgon Class monitor, which on 16th September 1918, while moored in Dover

Harbour close to the ammunition ship HMS *Gransha*, suffered a severe internal explosion followed by an uncontrollable fire. In order to avoid the extreme devastation that would have been caused had *Glatton*'s rear magazine exploded and set off *Gransha*'s cargo, the Port Commodore, Vice Admiral Sir Roger Keyes, ordered *Glatton* to be sunk (to extinguish the fire) by torpedoes from the destroyers HMS *Cossack* and HMS *Myngs*. This was done, although with difficulty as *Glatton* had been fitted with substantial anti-torpedo bulges. The Naval Court of Enquiry identified the failure of lagging between the 6-inch midship magazine and the boiler room as the probable cause of the disaster. The wreck was partially salvaged in 1926, and subsequently buried beneath the present car ferry terminal.

Of *Glatton*'s crew of some 300 men, 60 were killed immediately, and a further 19 died later from their burns. William was among those killed and he is commemorated at Woodlands Cemetery, Gillingham, as well as at the Portsmouth Naval Memorial. He was 21. The relatives notified of his death are listed as "widow, Jessie, 17 Nile Street, Emsworth and mother, Annie, 4 Garfield Road, Bishop's Waltham".

It is ironic that in 1913, during his pre-war service, William Copp served for some five months aboard HMS *Bulwark*. This vessel also exploded at her moorings at Sheerness in 1914, killing, among some 700 others, Edward Geoffrey Gunner, another of the men named on the Bishop's Waltham War Memorial (see under GUNNER).

William's widow Jessie married for a second time, to William Randall.

THE SERVICEMEN FROM BISHOP'S WALTHAM WHO DIED IN THE GREAT WAR

Garfield Road, where both Annie Copp, William's mother, and George Cottle's family lived

George James COTTLE (1882-1917)
In the Army Service Corps

On 9th September 1882 in Shedfield, George James Cottle was born to George Cottle and Alice Cottle (née Cleeve). The 1891 Census shows George junior, aged 8, living with his widowed father, aged 34, and his younger brother, Alfred, aged 4, in Forrest Road, Swanmore. His mother, Alice, had died early in 1887, perhaps at the birth of Alfred.

The 1901 Census shows George Cottle senior (now 44) and Alfred Cottle (14) both living at Ragleton Farm, Shedfield, with William Knight (farmer, employer and head of household) and his wife Eliza. A separate record reveals George Cottle (18) boarding with the Thornton family in East Grinstead. It seems possible that the death of Alice might have disturbed and dispersed the family.

George James served for a short period in the pre-war Royal Navy, as a Domestic 1c, No.364555, being described then as 5' 7" tall, with fair hair, blue eyes and a fair complexion. He joined HMS *Grafton* on 5th February 1906, subsequently transferred to HMS *Revenge* in August 1906, and was discharged to shore, at his own request, on 16th September of that year. Both vessels were acting as gunnery training ships at the time George was aboard.

On 12th June 1907, George married Daisy Florence Tilbury at St Peters, Southampton. The 1911 Census shows them living, aged 28 and 22 respectively, at 4 Clarence Terrace, Horton Road, Isleworth, Middlesex, with their first child, Gladys Ellen. George's occupation is given as "motor car driver, domestic". By 1915 they had moved back to Hampshire and were living in Garfield Road, Bishop's Waltham. The family had expanded to three children with the births of Stanley (September 1912) and Arthur George (April 1914).

George 's army records show that he joined the Army Service Corps (Mechanical Transport) at Winchester as Private No.281801 on 9th December 1915. The records are fire damaged but do record that he died, aged 34, at the Royal Herbert Hospital, Woolwich, on 20th February 1917. Originally admitted for German measles, George rapidly developed fatal bronchitis and broncho-pneumonia. He is buried in St Peter's Churchyard at Bishop's Waltham.

William John CUTLER (1897-1917)
Blacksmith's son killed near Ypres
William, son of James Cutler (blacksmith) and Mary Ann Cutler (née Hounsome), was born in 1897 in Bishop's Waltham, and was baptised in St Peter's Church on 5th December of that year. The 1901 Census shows him, aged 3, living with his parents and siblings (Charlotte, Lucy, Margaret and Arthur) in Free Street. By 1911 the family had moved to Bank Street – William was then 13 and at school, while another sister had been added, named Alice.

The National Roll of the Great War and the Register of UK Soldiers Died in the Great War record that William volunteered at Eastleigh in August 1914 (when he would have been 16) and joined the Hampshire Royal Garrison Artillery as Gunner No.352351. Probably because of his age, he remained in England until April 1916, when he was sent to France. About a year later, aged 19, he was killed in action near Ypres on 5th April 1917 and is buried at the Dickebusch New Military Cemetery, West Flanders, Belgium. His effects were sent to his mother, Mary Cutler.

James Cutler, the blacksmith, outside White Hart stables in Bank Street circa 1897, the year William was born

Cecil DAVIS (1889-1918)
Hambledon Hunt groom killed in France

Cecil Davis was born in 1889 in Meonstoke, son of Henry and Mary Ann Davis. The 1891 Census shows him, aged 2, living in Fry's Lane, Meonstoke, with his parents and siblings (Frank, Blanche and Ethel). In 1895 Cecil's father, Henry, died aged 58. The 1901 Census shows the family still living in Meonstoke, with Mary Ann now the Head of Household and Cecil at age

12. Cecil became an orphan at 17 on the death of his mother in 1906. The 1911 Census lists Cecil, now aged 22, as single and a groom working for the Hambledon Hunt, accommodated with two other hunt servants at The Kennels, Droxford. Towards the end of 1913, Cecil married Lilian Maud Fursey (the sister of William Arthur FURSEY, another of those named on the War Memorial) and a son, William Arthur, was born to them in 1914 – he lived to the good old age of 88.

Cecil Davis enlisted at Aldershot, probably in late 1914, in the Military Mounted Police as Private No.P/681. He was subsequently transferred to the Royal Warwickshire Regiment as Private No.43365, initially to the 16th Battalion and then to the 1st Battalion. He was sent to France on 29th August 1915, was killed in action in Flanders on 30th August 1918, aged 29, and was buried in the Vis-en-Artois British Cemetery, Haucourt, Nord-pas-de-Calais, France. He was entitled to the 1915 Star in addition to the usual Service and Victory medals. His effects were sent to his widow, Lilian.

In 1919 Lilian married again, to Albert E. Jacobs.

Albert Henry EMMETT (1889-1917)
Died in hospital in Malta
Albert Henry Emmett was born in 1889 in Upham, the seventh child of Henry Emmett, a farm labourer, and Mary Ann Emmett (née Abraham). The 1891 Census shows him, aged 2, living in the village of Upham, with his parents and six siblings. The next census lists the family at Sciviers Lane, Upham, and Albert has reached the age of 12. The 1911 Census reveals that Albert has left home, and is working as a groom at Captain Standish's Stables at Marwell Hall, Owlesbury. Early in1915 he married Ethel Mary Weavil, the event being recorded at the Droxford Registry Office.

Albert joined the 2nd Battalion of the Gloucestershire Regiment as Private No.22028 in 1915, and was sent to France on 21st July of that year. The unit was transferred to the Salonika theatre of war in late 1915, subsequently engaging in actions against the Bulgarian Army, including the capture of

Karajakois, and Yenikoi. Malaria and other illnesses proved a serious problem during the Salonika campaign. British non-battle casualties were over half a million, many of whom were transferred by ship to hospitals on the island of Malta. It seems likely that Albert was one of these, as the Register of Soldiers' Effects shows that he died on 20th February 1917, aged 28, in Malta. He was entitled to the 1915 Star, in addition to the usual Victory and Service medals. His effects were sent to his widow, Ethel. He is buried in the Pietà Military Cemetery, Northern Harbour, Malta.

Ethel remarried in about June of 1919, to Nathan Lacey. She died in 1962. There seem to have been no children from either marriage.

The community pump in Basingwell Street, where Alfred Emmett's family lived, circa 1914

Alfred Harry EMMETT (1894-1915)
From sweeping chimneys to Ypres
Alfred Harry Emmett, Rifleman Number B/1222 of the 9th Service Battalion of the Rifle Brigade, died in action in France at Hooge near Ypres on 31st

July 1915. He was 21. He volunteered in August 1914, and after a period of training was drafted to the Western Front later that year. His name is recorded on the Menin Gate Memorial. He was entitled to the 1914-15 Star in addition to the usual Service and Victory Medals.

Alfred was born to William and Eliza Jane Emmett (née Farrell) on 1st June 1894 in Bishop's Waltham, and was educated at Eastleigh Boys' School, later becoming an assistant chimney sweep in his father's business. The 1911 Census shows him, aged 16, living with his parents at Northam Road, Hedge End. At that time his parents had been married for 44 years and had produced 14 children, of who 13 were then still living.

Alfred must have had a busy family life, with his numerous brothers and sisters, but according to the entry in De Ruvigny's Roll of Honour he was himself unmarried. At the time of his death the same document gives the family address as Basingwell Street, Bishop's Waltham.

Louis EPPS (1894-1916)
From the Oxford and Cambridge Club to the Somme
George Epps and Honorah Louisa Boyce were both born in Bishop's Waltham in about 1864 and 1865 respectively. They married in 1893 and their first and only child, Louis, was born in 1894. The 1901 Census records the family: George, a gardener, Honorah Louisa, and Louis, then aged 7, living in Free Street, Bishop's Waltham. The 1911 Census shows that the family had moved further along Free Street to Albion Cottage (formerly occupied by George's parents), but that Louis had already left home and, aged 17, was working as the "service liftman" at The Oxford and Cambridge Club, 71-76 Pall Mall, London.

In July 1915 Louis Epps volunteered for the Army and joined the 1st Battalion the Hampshire Regiment as Private No.19167. In early 1916 he was drafted to France, where he joined a trench mortar battery. He was killed in action, aged 21, on 1st July 1916, the first day of the Battle of the Somme, when his battery came under heavy fire from German artillery. The War Diary for the 1st Battalion for that day describes an assault on the German trenches, resulting in many casualties and no gains. His name is inscribed on the Thiepval Memorial, Department de la Somme, Picardie, France. His effects were sent to his mother, Honorah.

Louis's father, George, died in 1927, but his mother survived until 1945.

Harry ETHERIDGE (1883-1919)
Dover Patrol Gunner

Born on 7th January 1883 in Bishopstoke, the son of George Etheridge (keeper of the Anchor Inn) and Ann Etheridge (née Hall), Harry is shown on the 1891 Census, aged 8, living with his mother and siblings in Basingwell Street, Bishop's Waltham. His father George had died in 1890. The 1901 Census records the family occupying a house in Houchin Street, but Harry is not with them. By then, he had already joined the Royal Navy, because the next Census, in 1911, shows Petty Officer 1st Class No.201408 Harry Etheridge (aged 28, born in Bishopstoke) on board HMS *Prince George* (a Majestic Class pre-Dreadnought battleship) anchored in Lyme Bay.

His Service Record shows that in fact he first entered the Navy at the age of 16, on 29th October 1898, and underwent training until he reached his 18th birthday on 7th January 1901, at which time he enlisted for 12 years (extended for a second term in 1913) as Ordinary Seaman No.201408. Over the following 14 years, whilst serving on various ships (including HMS *Aboukir, Barfleur, Prince George, Illustrious,* and *New Zealand*) and taking several courses at HMS *Excellent* – the Navy's gunnery school – he advanced steadily in rank to Petty Officer 1st Class. His Seaman's Record states that he "passed for gunner" on 2nd November 1914, was promoted Acting Gunner in February 1915, and was then transferred to the Officers Section.

Harry served as a Gunner initially on HMS *TB.027* (a torpedo boat), then on HMS *Surly* (a Rocket Class torpedo-boat destroyer) until 7th February

1918. Records show that he was "to be pensioned on 1st April 1918, physically unfit" and that he died "on 19th July 1919 from pulmonary tuberculosis".

Harry Etheridge's death in 1919, aged 36, is confirmed by the civil registration at Droxford in September 1919, and by his grave in St Peter's Churchyard, Bishop's Waltham. The grave is not a standard military type; it has a low railed enclosure and originally a cross, but the grave is now not in good order. It seems likely that he was discharged from the Naval Hospital at Haslar, and returned to his mother's house at 2 Albert Terrace before his death.

He was entitled to the 1914 Star, in addition to the usual Victory and British Service medals, and in March 1918 he was issued with a Silver War Badge.

Harry Etheridge's grave in St Peter's churchyard

Willian Arthur FURSEY (1896-1917)
From flowers to heavy guns

William John Fursey married Hannah Mary Stone at Frampton Parish Church, Dorset, on 28th April 1894. The 1901 Census shows the Fursey family, at that time consisting of William John aged 30, Hannah Mary (23), William Arthur (5) and Lilian Maud aged 2 (who later married Cecil DAVIS, also named on the Memorial), living in Church Street, West Coker, Somerset. By 1911 they had moved to Lower Lane, Bishop's Waltham, and William junior was working as a "gardener's lad" of 15.

William Arthur Fursey enlisted in Eastleigh as Gunner No.352323 in the 154th Heavy Battery of the Hampshire Royal Garrison Artillery (Territorial Force), and must have gone to France when the unit was sent there on 30th April 1916. He died of wounds on 19th June 1917 at the age of 21, and is buried at the Lijssenthoek Military Cemetery, Poperinge, Ypres, West Flanders, Belgium.

William Henry GARSIDE (1895-1917)
Killed at the Battle of Cambrai

William was born in Fareham between September and December 1895. The 1901 Census shows him, aged 5, living with his siblings and parents – Arthur Garside, a cycle fitter, and his wife Edith – at Bay Lodge, Spitalfield Lane, Chichester. Arthur and Edith, who had married in 1891, came from very different parts of England, Edith from St Pancras, Marylebone, and Arthur from Patricroft, Lancashire. Ten years later, in 1911, the family was living in Swanmore, Bishop's Waltham. William's occupation, at 15, is shown as a "market gardener (helping his father)", while Arthur, a little surprisingly, is said to be an "automobile engineer and market gardener".

In 1914 William enlisted at Gosport in the Hampshire Regiment as Private No.9488. He seems to have been transferred between the 1st and 2nd Battalions, but retained the same service number throughout. Interestingly his service number is only one different from that of William Edgar MAY (another of our war casualties) who was No.9489. They both enlisted at Gosport and may well have been friends. If such was the case, they were soon separated. William May went initially to the Balkans, while William Garside served in France from January 1915. He was killed in action on 21st November 1917, aged 22, probably at the Battle of Cambrai, which started on 20th November and continued until 7th December 1917. He was buried at the Marcoing British Cemetery, Nord-de-Pas-Calais, France, and was awarded the 1915 Star, as well as the standard Service and Victory Medals. His effects were sent to his mother, Edith.

Herbert GIBSON (1885-1914)
One of the "Old Contemptibles"[1]

The marriage of James Gibson and Mary Ann Cleaves was registered at Droxford in 1874. They had seven children, the fifth of whom was Herbert, born in 1885 in Swanmore. The 1891 Census records Herbert, aged 5, living with his parents and siblings in Chapel Road, Swanmore. His mother died in 1893, when he was 7. In 1901 he was listed at the Purbrook Industrial School at Farlington. Herbert was about 22 when his father died in 1907. The 1911 Census shows him at the Royal Field Artillery, Bulford Hut Barracks, Bulford Camp, near Salisbury.

There is a record, in the Royal Navy Register of Seamen's Services, of a Herbert Gibson, born in Swanmore in 1885, joining the Navy as a stoker (No.307341) in September 1904, and being discharged in 1908 as "of no value to the Service" after serving for just over three rather "colourful" years, during which his character assessment deteriorated rapidly from "good" to "indifferent", and he spent some six spells doing hard labour or in the cells. This might possibly be "our" Herbert, who, according to the censuses, was at school in 1901 and in the Artillery in 1911, leaving a suitable gap for wild oats to be sown.

Herbert's Army Service Records seem to have been destroyed in WWII, but other documents show that he enlisted at Gosport, as Gunner

[1] The Old Contemptibles were members of the British Expeditionary Force that served in Flanders right at the start of the war, between 5th August and 22nd November. At the first battle of Ypres, their stand against a force ten times their number prevented the German advance against the Channel ports.

No.58034, in the 32nd Battery of the 33rd Brigade of the Royal Field Artillery, probably in about 1910. He arrived in France on 6th November 1914 and died of wounds on 28th of that month, aged 29. He is buried at the Merville Communal Cemetery, Nord-Pas-de-Calais, France. In addition to the usual Victory and Service medals, Herbert was entitled to the 1914 Star and clasp.

Herbert had married Kathleen Askew in 1914 and his effects were sent to her at Bank Street, Bishop's Waltham. A boy, Herbert G. Gibson, was born to Kathleen in 1915 (his birth being registered at Droxford) some months after his father's death.

Walter Gibson, Herbert's younger brother, also married into the Askew family. His wedding with Ellen Askew took place in March 1916. The Askews kept the bakery shop in Bank Street for many years.

Neil Stewart GIBSON (1891-1917)
Served in India and Mesopotamia

Born in Portsmouth to Harry Gibson and Isabella Gibson (née Stewart), Neil Stewart Gibson (their only child) is shown in the 1891 Census, at 2 months old, living with his parents at 18 Fredington Street. The 1901 Census records the family at The George Inn, West Meon where Neil's father, Harry, was the publican. By 1911 the Gibsons had moved to Whitchurch, where Harry was the innkeeper of The Prince Regent. Neil was then 20 and listed as an "indoor manservant".

Neil enlisted at Winchester, probably in September 1914, as Private No.201054, in the 1st/4th Territorial Force Battalion of the Hampshire Regiment. This unit sailed for India on 9th October 1914, reaching Karachi by 11th November, and was amalgamated into the 2nd (Rawalpindi) Division in January 1915. On 18th March 1915 the Battalion landed at Basra, in Iraq, and remained in Mesopotamia for the rest of the War. Neil Gibson had reached the rank of corporal before he died, aged 24, on 26th December 1917. He is buried in Baghdad, at the North Gate War Cemetery.

Casualties from disease were very high in the Mesopotamian campaign. Cholera, typhoid and malaria were rife. Indeed General Maud, the Commander, died of cholera only about a month before Neil's death. It seems likely that Neil died from one of these diseases.

There are some anomalies in the records. The index of UK Soldiers Died in the Great War confirms his birth place as Portsmouth, and his place of residence as Upham, Hampshire, while the War Graves Commission names his parents as Harry and Isabella Gibson, of Tichbourne Cottage, Fair Oak, Eastleigh. In the 1901 Census, however, Neil's mother's name was given as Jane rather than Isabella. This is probably an enumerator error arising from the presence of her sister Jane, who was a visitor on the census day. The War Memorial dedication ceremony list gives his name as Neil Stuart Gibson.

Robin George Bruce GIFFARD-BRINE (1899-1916)
Midshipman on HMS *Invincible* at Jutland

Robin was born in Bishop's Waltham on 3rd Feb 1899, the third son of George Augustus Giffard and Eleanor Rosalie Giffard (née Brine) of Highfield, Winchester Road. His father, a Royal Navy Captain at the time of Robin's birth, went on to have an illustrious career, commanding various naval vessels (including the pre-Dreadnought battleship HMS *Hannibal*), reaching the rank of Admiral, and becoming Superintendent of the Chatham Dockyard, before he retired in 1913. The Brine family were prominent in the Army and the Church, but more so in the Navy – their entry in *Burke's Families* commences with James Brine, Admiral of the White.

Robin was at school in Twyford at the time of the 1911 Census. Subsequently he joined the Royal Navy and by August 1914 had become a midshipman. He served in that capacity in 1915 on HMS *Hindustan* (a pre-Dreadnought battleship), and later on HMS *Invincible* (a 17,000-ton battle cruiser). He was killed in action when *Invincible* became one of the 14 Royal Navy vessels sunk at the Battle of Jutland on 31st May 1916. He was only 17. Robin was entitled to the 1915 Star, in addition to the usual Victory and Service medals, and is remembered on a brass plaque in St Peter's Church and on the Portsmouth Naval Memorial.

Rear Admiral Sir Horace Lambert Alexander Hood KCB DSO MVO, whose name is read out on each Remembrance Sunday at St Mary's, Upham, was also killed on *Invincible* at Jutland. *Invincible* was struck by numerous shells from the three salvoes each fired upon her by the German ships SMS *Lutzow* and *Derfflinger*, and sank almost immediately, with a loss of 1,026 lives – only six of her crew survived. The wreck was found after the War by a Royal Navy minesweeper, and the location is a protected site under the Protection of Military Remains Act, 1986.

The Alberta-British Columbia Boundary Survey, which worked in the Canadian Rockies from 1913 to 1925, named a number of previously unidentified peaks for British warships lost in the Great War, among them Mount Invincible.

Midshipman Robin Giffard-Brine

Edward/Patrick GORE (1901-1917)
Young sailor – died at 16

Edward/Patrick Gore was born on 9th March 1901 in Portsmouth, son of John Gore, a Chief Stoker in the Royal Navy, and Elizabeth Gore (née Hockey). He is recorded in the 1901 Census as 1 month old and living with his mother and three of his siblings at 33 Cranleigh Road, Portsmouth. At that time his father, John, was serving in HMS *Monarch* in Simons Bay, Cape of Good Hope. By 1911 he is shown, with three siblings and both his parents, Elizabeth and John, now a naval pensioner and publican, at The Fir Tree Inn, Upham (the building is now a substantial private house). Also in 1911, his eldest sister, Marguerite (Maggie) Gore, married another of those listed on the Bishop's Waltham War Memorial – William MATTHEWS.

Having attended the Royal Hospital School at Greenwich (often called "The Cradle of the Navy"), Edward/Patrick enlisted in the Royal Navy in September 1916, as a boy entrant. In March of the following year he entered a 12 year engagement as a trainee telegraphist. At this time he was described as 5' 2" tall, with dark hair, brown eyes and a ruddy complexion. He joined one of the Dover Patrol's Tribal Class destroyers, HMS *Tartar*, on 4th June 1917. Tragically, less than a fortnight later, on 17th June, he was killed aged only 16 when *Tartar* struck a mine in the English Channel.

The vessel was very severely damaged – the bows and bridge being completely destroyed – but nevertheless she was kept afloat and repaired, and survived the War, being sold for scrap in 1921. A diary note by a naval officer based in Dover reported: "*Tartar* came into Dover on 18th June 1917 – struck a mine while escorting a troopship – nearly all hands killed."

Edward is so named on some documents, and as Patrick on others. However, continuities between the mother's identity and birthplace, and his ages, suggest, quite strongly, that Edward and Patrick was one and the same person.

THE GUNNER BROTHERS
The Family

The Gunner family was, for many years, very prominent in Bishop's Waltham and the Meon Valley as bankers and solicitors, and benefactors to the local churches. Peter Watkins' excellent book *Bishop's Waltham, Parish, Town and Church* devotes a whole chapter (Ch. 10) to them.

Ridgemede House, the family home of the Gunners

At the beginning of the Great War Charles Richard Gunner (1853-1934) was living in Bishop's Waltham with his wife, Jessie Kate (née Mason), at Ridgemede, the house he had built in 1897 (now a care home). Since their marriage in 1880, nine children had been born to them: two girls (Daisy May and Elizabeth Margaret) and seven boys (Charles James, John Hugh, Thomas Ridge, Walter Robin, Richard Humphrey, Benjamin George, and Edward Geoffrey). Of the seven boys, three had already died: Charles James in 1893 of illness while at school; Thomas Ridge in 1910 while serving with the Northumberland Fusiliers in India; and Richard Humphrey in 1888, shortly after birth. Tragically, three of the Gunners' four remaining sons were to lose their lives during the 1914-18 War. Only Walter Robin survived – he died in 1973.

Sub-Lieutenant Edward Geoffrey Gunner

THE SERVICEMEN FROM BISHOP'S WALTHAM WHO DIED IN THE GREAT WAR

Edward Geoffrey GUNNER (1894-1914)
Lost in the *Bulwark* explosion

Edward was born in 1894. He attended Dartmouth Naval College from 1908 and joined the Royal Navy in 1911. Having served as a midshipman on HMS *Bellerophon*, he was transferred when he was 20 as a sub-lieutenant to HMS *Bulwark*. This vessel, a 16,000-ton pre-Dreadnought battleship, blew up at her moorings near Sheerness, in the estuary of the River Medway, on 26th November 1914. The catastrophe took the lives of all but 12 of the complement of 750. No officers survived. The naval court of enquiry decided that the explosion was probably caused by the storage of cordite charges too close to an engine room bulkhead. Edward is commemorated on the Portsmouth Naval Memorial.

Benjamin George GUNNER M.C. (1892-1915)
Holder of the Military Cross

Within less than a year, the Gunner family had to withstand another bereavement when Captain Benjamin George Gunner M.C., serving with the 1st Battalion of the Northumberland Fusiliers, was killed in action on 7th October 1915 near Ypres. He was 23. The Battalion's War Diary says, "at about 5.45 p.m. Captain and Adjutant B. G. Gunner was killed outside the battalion headquarters by a stray bullet." He was mentioned in despatches on 22nd June 1915, and the *London Gazette* for 23rd June recorded the award of his Military Cross, while that of 16th November showed his promotion to Captain with effect from 21st August. It has not been possible to find either the recommendation or the citation for his M.C. He is buried at the Brandhoek Military Cemetery, West-Vlaanderen, Belgium.

Born in 1892, Benjamin was educated at Twyford School and Marlborough College, before going on to Sandhurst in 1911. He showed his athleticism at all three establishments. Having obtained a commission in the Northumberland Fusiliers, he joined the Regiment in India in 1912, subsequently being transferred with his battalion to France on SS *Norman* in August 1914. In all probability he joined The Northumberland Fusiliers (The Fighting Fifth) because it was his elder brother's regiment. Sadly, Lieutenant Thomas Ridge Gunner had died of enteric fever (typhoid) in 1910, before Benjamin arrived in India.

Captain John Hugh Gunner

John Hugh GUNNER (1884-1918)
Played cricket for Hampshire

The end of the War was only three months away when 34 year old Captain John Hugh Gunner of the Hampshire Carabiniers Yeomanry died on 9th August 1918 from wounds sustained at Kemmel, Belgium. He had been commissioned into the Yeomanry in 1904 and retired in early 1914, but rejoined at the outbreak of war. He is buried at La Clytte Military Cemetery, Heuvelland, in Belgium.

John was born on 17th May 1884 at Bishop's Waltham, the second son of Charles and Jessie Gunner. He was educated at Marlborough and Trinity College Cambridge. Inspired, no doubt, by his father's love of cricket, he captained the Marlborough College cricket team in 1902, represented Trinity College Cambridge, and played for Hampshire in six first class matches, including one against the West Indies in 1906. He joined his father in the family firm of solicitors.

John was married. His wedding to Dorothy Kirby took place in 1909, and the couple are recorded by the 1911 Census as living with their 5 month old son, John Paul Gunner, in Winchester Street, Botley. A second son, Geoffrey Hamilton Gunner, was born in 1915, and the family moved house to Warren Road, Bournemouth. After John's death the family moved again, to Kingsgate Street, Winchester. Both his sons joined the Royal Navy before the outbreak of World War II and served throughout that war. His wife Dorothy died in 1968, aged 86.

Charlie HAMMOND (1877-1916)
Casualty of the battle of the Somme
Charlie was born in Swanmore in 1877, the fifth son of Obed Hammond and Anne Hammond (née Pink), who were married on 28th March 1869 at St Mary's, Portsea. Both the 1881 and 1891 Censuses show the Hammond family living in Vicarage Road, Swanmore, but by 1901 they had moved to Free Street, Bishop's Waltham. The 1911 Census records Charlie, then 34, still living there with his parents, the only one of their children still at home.

Charlie, who was about 37 when the War began, enlisted at Winchester in the 14th Service Battalion of the Hampshire Regiment as Private No.20806. The unit had been formed at Portsmouth on 3rd September 1914, adopted by the War Office in May 1915 and landed in France at Le Havre on 6th March 1916. Charlie was killed in action on 3rd September 1916, aged 39, during the battle of the Somme – an action that lasted from July to November 1916. His name is inscribed on the Thiepval Memorial, Picardie, France. His effects were sent to his father, Obed.

Both Charlie and his father, Obed, have forenames that seem not to be "proper" names, but many of the documents available on the internet use just those names. It may be that Obed is not merely a diminutive for Obadiah, but a name in its own right, and Charlie was perhaps Obed's son's actual official name, rather than Charles.

Free Street, where Charlie Hammond lived, circa 1912

Herbert HAMMOND (1886-1917)
A career Naval man

Herbert was born in 1886 in Bishop's Waltham to Henry Hammond and Sarah Hammond (née Conduct), and appears in both the 1891 and 1901 Censuses, living with his parents and siblings in Waltham Chase.

THE SERVICEMEN FROM BISHOP'S WALTHAM WHO DIED IN THE GREAT WAR

On 24th September 1902, giving his age as 18, Herbert enlisted in the Royal Marines Light Infantry, Portsmouth Division, as Private No.12522. Some years later, on 22nd February 1907, he signed up for 12 years in the Royal Navy, and was given a new Service Number: 311462. His Seaman's Service Record shows his former membership of the Marines, and describes him as 5' 7" tall, with brown hair, grey eyes and a fresh complexion. The 1911 Census lists him as serving on HMS *Illustrious*, at Portland. His marriage to May Cawdrey in the fourth quarter of 1914 is recorded in the Births Marriages and Deaths Index for Fareham. He served on numerous ships before joining the company of HMS *Partridge* as a stoker 1st Class on 1st July 1916. *Partridge* was a new M Class destroyer, built by Swan Hunter, and launched only three months earlier.

On 11th December 1917 a British convoy left Lerwick in the Shetlands bound for Bergen in Norway. There were six merchant ships, mostly small Scandinavian-owned vessels (*Bollsta, Bothnia, Cordova, Torlief, Kong Magnus* and *Maracaibo*), while the naval escort consisted of the destroyers HMS *Pellew* and *Partridge*, and four very lightly armed trawler/minesweepers (*Tokio, Commander Fullerton, Livingstone,* and *Lord Alverstone*).

The following day the convoy was intercepted close to the Norwegian coast by four German destroyers (*G.101, G.103, G.104* and *V.100*). The German boats were larger and more heavily armed than either *Partridge* or *Pellew*. The German Commander (Lt. Comm. H. Kolbe) ordered three of his vessels to engage the British destroyers and the fourth to sink the trawlers and merchant ships. *Partridge* was hit by both shell fire and torpedoes, and sank almost immediately. Though suffering engine room damage, *Pellew* managed to escape into the mist of a squall, the sole survivor of the convoy. She was later towed into Selbjorn Fiord by a Norwegian ship. *Partridge* had a crew of 121, of whom 24 were picked up by German vessels and became prisoners of war, and 97 were either killed during the battle or drowned in the aftermath. Herbert, then aged 31, was one of these.

He is commemorated on the Portsmouth Naval Memorial, and is entitled to the 1915 Star, in addition to the usual Service and Victory Medals.

Herbert's widow, May Hammond, contracted a second marriage in 1919 at Droxford, to Ewart W. Russell.

Frederick William HARVELL (1889-1917)
With the Hampshire Regiment in Salonika

Frederick was born in Bishop's Waltham in 1889, son of Charles John Harvell and Jane Harvell (née New). The 1901 Census shows him, aged 11, living at Primrose Terrace, Beeches Hill, with his mother and younger brother, Jesse. By 1911 Jane (now shown as a widow) had moved to Bank Street and is listed together with her daughter Mary Jane and younger son, Jesse.

There is no trace of Frederick in Britain in 1911, but there is a shipping passenger record of a Fred Harvell, (a farm labourer, English address Bank Street, Bishop's Waltham) landing from the SS *Corsican* at Liverpool on 14th December 1915 from St Johns, New Brunswick, Canada. It seems likely that Frederick William was in Canada at the time of the 1911 Census, but decided to come home to join up.

In 1915 Frederick volunteered for the Army at Winchester, joining the 12th Service Battalion of the Hampshire Regiment as Private No.22309. He was sent to Salonika, and took part in many engagements on the Macedonian Front. He died of wounds on 17th April 1917, aged 28, and is buried in the Karasouli Military Cemetery, Polykastro, Kilkis, Central Macedonia, Greece. His effects were sent to his mother, Jane.

Frederick's younger brother, Jesse, also served with the Hampshire Regiment as Private No.18166. He was in France for three years or so, and took part in the battles of Ypres, the Somme, Arras and Cambrai, but survived the war and was demobilised in 1919.

Howard Dudley HEWETT (1896-1918)
An Officer in the Buffs and the Royal Flying Corps

Edward William Hewett and Ada Lavinia King married in 1892. Howard, their second son, was born in Bishop's Waltham on 6th May 1896. The 1901 Census reports Howard, aged 4, living with his parents and three brothers in Portland Square, Bishop's Waltham (now the site of the Lower Lane Car Park). By 1911 when Howard was 14, the family had moved to Forrest Road, Swanmore, and the Census shows that Edward (an auctioneer) and Ada had six children – four sons and two daughters, with twin boys having been born in 1901 and twin girls in 1909.

Although the family seems to have had no obvious connection with Kent, Howard joined the 1st Battalion of the East Kent Regiment (usually called The Buffs) as a 2nd Lieutenant, but subsequently transferred, at the rank of Lieutenant, to 13h Squadron of the Royal Flying Corps/RAF. This squadron was formed in January 1915 and was primarily involved in Army co-operation duties, and later in bombing raids. His British Army Medal Index Cards and Rolls record show his membership of both the Army and the Air Force, and include reference to correspondence with his father, E.W. Hewett of Waiwera, Winchester Road, Bishop's Waltham.

The list of UK Soldiers Died in the Great War states that he died of wounds, two weeks before the end of the war, on 27th October 1918, aged 20. This date is corroborated by an entry in the National Probate Calendar, which adds that his death took place at the 59th Casualty Clearing Station, Awoingt, France. Administration of his Will was granted to his father. He is buried at the Awoingt British Cemetery, Nord-Pas-de-Calais, France.

William John HEWETT (1877-1915)
Local house-builder killed at Aubers Ridge

Captain William John Hewett of the 2nd Battalion of the Royal Munster Fusiliers was killed in action on 9th May 1915, aged 38, at Aubers Ridge near Richebourg St Vaast, Pas de Calais, France. He is buried at the Cabaret-Rouge cemetery at Souchez. His Medal Roll cards show that he went out to France with the British Expeditionary Force in 1914, and was entitled to the 1914 Star, in addition to the usual Victory and British Service Medals. Correspondence in connection with his medals was conducted with his widow, at Strathavon, Crown Hill, Bishop's Waltham.

During the evening of 8th May their chaplain, Father Francis Gleeson, held a service for the Fusiliers, which is the subject of a fine painting by Fortunino Matania called "The Last General Absolution of the Munsters at Rue de Bois". At 5am the next day the Munster Fusiliers – part of a much larger British force – went over the top and advanced, behind a creeping barrage laid down by British artillery, towards the German trenches. Despite heavy casualties from German shelling and machine gun fire, the Fusiliers bravely continued to move forward, some actually breaching the German lines and planting one of their green company standards on the parapet. Other elements of the attack had, however, gone badly wrong and at 10.30am the Fusiliers were ordered to retire. During the retreat they suffered further casualties from misdirected British artillery fire, and when they reached their own trenches were found to have lost 500 of the 700 men who had started out that morning. This action, known as the Battle of Aubers Ridge, was part of the 2nd Battle of Artois, which started on 9th May and went on until 18th June 1915.

The Royal Munster Fusiliers Association held ceremonies in May 2015 at the sites of the absolution and of the battle itself. Matania's original painting was destroyed by fire during WWII, but many reproductions were made during the period between the wars.

"The Last General Absolution of the Munsters at Rue de Bois" by Fortunino Matania

William had been born in 1877 in Bishop's Waltham, to Edward William Hewett and Anne Elizabeth Hewett. He appears in the 1881, 1891, 1901 and 1911 Censuses for Bishop's Waltham, and in the last two is shown with his wife, Florence Ella Hewett (née Payne). They married in 1897 and had three children, of whom two were still living at the time of the 1911 Census, when William was 34 years old, living in Coppice Hill, and described as a "house builder". It is likely that he was the uncle of Howard Dudley HEWETT (although this cannot be verified without further research).

Francis HIGGINS (1891-1917)
Killed after just two months at the Western Front

The 1891 Census shows that Francis Higgins was born at East Woodhay, near Newbury, in that year, to Charles and Mary Jane Higgins. By 1901, Francis, aged 10, was living with his parents and three sisters at 3 Vernon Hill Cottages, Bishop's Waltham. His father was then, probably, acting as gardener to Lieutenant General Elrington of Vernon Hill House. In 1911 the family was living in Basingwell Street, with only their youngest daughter still at home. Francis had married Kate Miles earlier in the year and was living with his new bride at Fontley, near Fareham.

Francis volunteered for the Army in May 1915, initially joining the Hampshire Regiment as Private No.280043. Subsequently he was transferred to the 2/8th Battalion of the Worcester Regiment and given the new service No.260253. He was sent to France in June 1917, and was killed in action in Belgium, aged 26, on 27th August 1917. He is buried at the Ypres Town Cemetery Extension. His effects were sent to his widow, Kate, who was then living at Corhampton, near Droxford.

The Higgins family with Francis standing behind his parents

Andrew Buchanan KING (1875-1915)
A Scottish officer killed at Ypres

Major Andrew Buchanan King was an officer in the 7th Battalion of the Argyll and Sutherland Highlanders. The unit was involved in heavy fighting near Ypres, and on the 2nd May 1915 Major King personally led a charge through gas to retake some trenches, preventing their use by the enemy for an advance. On 24th May, during a heavy German bombardment towards the end of the 2nd battle of Ypres, he was struck by shrapnel while tending some of his wounded men. He was taken to No.10 Casualty Clearing Station at

Hazebrouck, where he died on 28th May, aged 40. He had been serving in the Expeditionary Force in France and Flanders from December 1914, and was known as a brave and popular officer.

Andrew was born in Glasgow on 17th March 1875, the third child of Colonel Charles Mackintosh King and Jane Margaret King (née Buchanan). He was educated at St Ninian's, Moffat, and Fettes College, and joined the 4th Stirlingshire Volunteers (which later became the Argyll and Sutherland Highlanders) in 1897, rising to the rank of Major by 1911. Before the outbreak of War he was the Unionist candidate for Stirlingshire, and on 17th April 1912, at St Thomas Church, Newport, Isle of Wight, he married Evelyn Nina Sharpe, the second daughter of the Rev. Henry Edmund Sharpe M.A., then vicar of Newport, who later became the rector of Bishop's Waltham (1913-1931).

Andrew and Evelyn had two children, the first, Nina Margaret, born on 5th February 1913, lived until 1997, while the second, Charles Andrew, born on 25th July 1915, lived until 2002. Evelyn herself remarried, becoming Mrs Crombie.

Memorial plaque to Major King in St Peter's church

As well as the name on the War Memorial, there is a brass plaque on the wall of St Peter's Church commemorating Major King (see below). He was entitled to the 1914 Star as well as the usual Victory and Service Medals.

Henry Percy Walter LACEY (1894-1916)
Killed in phosgene gas attack
Henry, third son of William Lacey and Mary Jane Lacey (née Jeffery), was born in 1894 in Waltham Chase. The Census for 1901 shows him, then aged 7, with his parents and six siblings, still living in Waltham Chase. His father William died in 1903 and his mother entered into her second marriage, to Ernest Sheppard, in 1904. The 1911 Census records Henry, now 17 and working as a groom, as living with his mother and stepfather, and three of his blood siblings (Arthur, Mary and Frederick) in St Peter's Street, Bishop's Waltham. Henry was usually known as Harry.

Choir boy Harry Lacey outside St Peter's Church

In August 1914 Harry joined the Hampshire Regiment as Private No.9169. Initially he was with the 1st Battalion, which arrived in France at Le Havre on 23rd August 1914. Subsequently he was promoted to Corporal and, after the 2nd Battalion arrived at the Western Front (from Gallipoli/Egypt) on 23rd April 1916, appears to have been transferred to that unit.

He was killed in action on 9th August 1916, aged 22, and is buried at the Potijze (also spelt Pottize) Chateau Wood Cemetery, West Flanders, Belgium. Henry died as a result of the gas attack that took place on the night of 8-9th August. An entry on the website for Potijze cemetery reads: "On 9 August 1916, as the Somme offensive raged further South, the 1st and 2nd Battalions of the Hampshire Regiment spent ten days in trenches just east of the chateau. As they were preparing to leave, the Germans staged a surprise attack using a potent form of phosgene gas. Both units were caught unawares, and although no ground was conceded, the Regiment suffered over 240 casualties, about half of whom were killed." The 2nd Battalion's own War Diary refers to the gas as being "of a particularly deadly kind". In addition to the usual Victory and British Service Medals, Henry was entitled to the 1914 Star.

Henry's platoon commander, Lieutenant Alfred Tilley, wrote a personal letter of commiseration to his mother, Mary Jane Lacey/Sheppard. Alfred Tilley was himself of interest, having joined the 15th Hussars as a private in 1907 and been promoted to 2nd Lieutenant in 1916 – presumably he was one of the "Old Contemptibles" (see footnote on page 58). A few days after he wrote the letter to Henry's mother, he was himself wounded and disappeared from the War Diary. He survived the war, appeared on the 1939 Register and seemingly died in 1955.

Henry Lacey and William MAY were both corporals in the 2nd Battalion of the Hampshires . The 1911 Census shows them living quite close to each other in Bishop's Waltham (Henry in St Peter's Street, William in Houchin Street). They most probably knew one another, may even have been friends, and fought and died together.

August 13th 1916.

2nd Hampshire Regt
B E F
France

Dear Mrs Lacey
It is with much regret that I have to inform you, of your Son Cpl Lacey. death from Gas Poisoning, I am indeed Sorry and mourn with you in his loss, He was a splended fellow the best man that I had in my platoon and was looking forward to the time when he would be promoted, He would have been by now, if he had lived, but he died An Hero every inch of him, Every thing that I could possibly do was done for him, but all to no purpose, He died as he lived a Briton every inch of him, How I wish that we could have saved him for your Sake as well as ours he refused to leave us telling me every time that I spoke to him that he was quite alright and I could not get him away from the trenches untill I gave him an order to leave us, but it was too late then Madam you have had a Son worth a dozen Germans and I hope that you bear up in your Sad loss I remain
Yours truely
A Tilley Lt.

Letter of commiseration to Harry Lacey's mother from Lieutenant Alfred Tilley

THE SERVICEMEN FROM BISHOP'S WALTHAM WHO DIED IN THE GREAT WAR

Ernest Edward LEE (1882-1917)
A young man "adopted" by a local photographer

Information about Ernest's birth, parentage and very early life is elusive, although an approximate date and place of birth (about 1882 and Southampton) can be deduced from the censuses.

The young Ernest is recorded by the 1891 Census as a visitor (aged eight and a scholar) at the home of Paul and Annie Desa in School Hill, Bishop's Waltham. The next Census (1901) lists Ernest as a boarder, again with the Desas, then living in Brook Street. It almost seems as though the Desas (a long-married but childless couple) had unofficially adopted Ernest. Paul Desa was a professional photographer, originally from the Isle of Wight, and was listed in the Bishop's Waltham section of Kellys Directory in 1911 as a photographer and shop keeper in Red Lion Street. In that year Paul Desa was 74 and his wife ten years younger.

The England & Wales Marriage Index (FreeBMD) shows that Ernest and Fanny Olive Stone were married at South Stoneham, near Southampton, in 1908 and the 1911 Census indicates that the Desas continued their "sponsorship", with Ernest listed once more as a boarder, but now together with Fanny and their three children (Hilda aged 2, Lucy 1, and Ernest junior "just born"). Apparently, on Ernest's death, his widow returned with their children to the Christchurch area, where she died in 1936 aged 51.

The Register of UK Soldiers Died in the Great War records that Ernest joined the 1st Battalion of the Hampshire Regiment in 1915, at Winchester, as Private No.15243, and that he died of wounds on 10th April 1917 in France, aged 35. He was buried at Étaples Military Cemetery, Nord-pas-de-Calais, France. His Medal Index Card states that he was sent to the Balkans in July 1915. Subsequently the battalion was transferred to France and at some stage Ernest was moved to the 2nd Battalion. He was entitled to the 1915 Star, in addition to the usual Service and Victory Medals.

George LOVELL (1880-1916)
At Jutland on HMS Indefatigable

George Lovell was born in 1880 in Exton to William John Lovell and Elizabeth Lovell (née Earwaker). The 1881 Census shows George, aged 7 months, with his parents and elder brother at Gatcombe Farm, Exton. By 1891 the family had moved to Strete End near Ashton, Bishop's Waltham, and in 1901 the family were living at 3 Primrose Terrace, Beeches Hill, Bishop's Waltham. At that time George, then aged 20, was working as a "carter on farm". The 1911 census showed that the Lovells had moved again, but only a short distance, to 2 Margaret Cottages, Beeches Hill but by that time George had left home.

In fact George had joined the Royal Marines Artillery in 1906, as Gunner No.11884. By 1916 he was serving in HMS *Indefatigable*, an 18,500-ton battle cruiser launched in 1909. He was killed in action at the Battle of Jutland on 31st May 1916, aged 36, when *Indefatigable* was destroyed in two catastrophic explosions.

According to the official history, "the duel between *Indefatigable* and the *Von der Tann* had been growing in intensity till, a few minutes after 4.00, the British ship was suddenly hidden in a burst of flame and smoke. A salvo of three shots had fallen on her upper deck and must have penetrated to a magazine. She staggered out of line, sinking by the stern when another salvo struck her; she turned over in a moment and all trace of her was gone."

Indefatigable had a crew of 1,019, of which only two survived. The wreck is now protected from disturbance by the Protection of Military Remains Act 1986. In addition to the inscription on the Bishop's Waltham War Memorial, George is commemorated on the Portsmouth Naval Memorial.

The Alberta-British Columbia Boundary Survey began work in 1913 and continued every summer until 1925. Many of the previously unnamed peaks were given names related to WWI – Mount Indefatigable was named after the lost battle cruiser.

William MATTHEWS (1884-1915)
Professional soldier in the Royal Engineers

William Matthews was born in Owslebury on 10th May 1884 and baptised in the Parish Church on 6th September 1885, the son of Henry and Emily Kate Matthews. By 1891 the family are shown (William now aged 6) living at Black Down, Owslebury. The 1901 Census reveals that they have moved to the Lane End part of the village of Cheriton, near Alresford, and there are seven children – William, at 16, is a "general labourer on farm".

On the day of the Census in 1911 William was staying with his parents and two younger sisters at Longwood Dean, near Winchester, and his occupation is given as "soldier". In fact William had been a soldier for some eight years by then. He had enlisted at Guildford on 24th November 1903 at the age of 19 years and 5 months, in the 12th Company of the Royal Engineers, as Sapper No.13152. He married Marguerite Gore (see photo on page 9), on 26th December 1911, with the ceremony being witnessed by his sister Dora Matthews and a William Oliver. There seems to have been only one child of this marriage, William John, who was born on 8th June 1914 in Ropley. Marguerite was the elder sister of another of those named on the Bishop's Waltham War Memorial, Edward/Patrick GORE. The Matthews and Gores must have been well acquainted.

William's British Army Service Records are reasonably comprehensive and well preserved. They show him to have been of exemplary character, and to have become an expert stationary steam-engine driver. They also list his pre-marriage next of kin, conclusively tying the army records to the censuses.

Initially he served in England for about two years, successfully passing various courses (including two at the Royal Engineering School of Submarine Mining at Portsmouth), and then in September 1905 he was sent to Malta, where he spent some five and a half years. He returned to England in 1911 and was transferred to the Reserves later that year. At the outbreak of the War he was recalled, and went to France with the British Expeditionary Force on 8th September 1914. He was posted missing on 9th August 1915, aged 31, that date being subsequently accepted by the authorities as his date of death. He received the 1914 Star as well as the British War and Victory medals. In addition to his inscription on the Bishop's Waltham War Memorial, he is commemorated on the Menin Gate, at Ypres.

War Office letters, dated 1916, in connection with William's pension (15 shillings a week for a widow and one child) were addressed to his widow, Marguerite, at two addresses, Old Mill Villa, Owslebury, and 4 Primrose Cottages, Beeches Hill, Bishop's Waltham.

William's connection with the R.E. Submarine Mining School is interesting. The responsibility of the R.E. Submarine Mining Service (which was set up as part of the Army in the 1860s) was to defend British ports and naval bases by means of searchlights, guns and underwater explosive devices (ie mines) operated from the shore. In order to install fixed mines and their control wires, the R.E. submarine miners had to be proficient, among other things, in small boat handling, diving and electrical work. Their working uniform was very similar to that of a Royal Navy sailor, featuring a round cap without a peak, and a pea jacket. It seems possible that the photograph (right) of William, taken in Malta, is of him in the R.E. Submarine Miners' working uniform. After 1905 the Government decided to do away with the shore-controlled mine and searchlight defences for the UK rivers and estuaries, and the Navy progressively took over responsibility for sea mining.

William Matthews with a stationary steam engine

William Edgar MAY (1895-1916)
A survivor of Gallipoli who died in a phosgene gas attack in France

William's parents, William Thomas May and Emily Woodhatch, may well have been childhood sweethearts. Certainly they were neighbours, shown by the 1881 Census to have been living in adjacent houses in Lime Kiln Lane, Dean, Bishop's Waltham. They married in 1883 and William Edgar, their fifth child, was born in 1895. By 1901 William Edgar was 6, and living with his parents and siblings at Strete End, Bishop's Waltham, while the 1911 Census shows him in Houchin Street.

The National Roll of the Great War states that William was already in the 2nd Battalion of the Hampshire Regiment at the outbreak of war, and that he was drafted with that unit to Gallipoli in April 1915, landing at Suvla Bay, where he was wounded. After the evacuation of Gallipoli he was transferred to France. He was promoted to corporal but the date of his promotion is not known. William was killed in action on 9th August 1916, aged 21, as the result of a large scale surprise gas attack involving both the 1st and 2nd Battalions of the Hampshires. He is buried at the Potijze Burial Ground Cemetery, West Flanders, Belgium. In addition to the Victory and British Service Medals, William was entitled to the 1915 Star.

William May and Henry Lacey were both corporals in the 2nd Battalion of the Hampshires. Both were killed on the same day in a surprise attack by the Germans. They lived quite close to each other in Bishop's Waltham, William in Houchin Street, and Henry in St Peter's Street, so it seems very likely that they knew one another, and might well have been friends. A more detailed description of this attack is given in the entry for Henry LACEY.

Corporal William May (middle of back row)

Walter MEARS (1887-1916)
On HMS *Lion* at Jutland

Although his name does not appear on the Bishop's Waltham War Memorial (or on the Rolls of Honour), Walter Mears seems to have all the qualifications required for both. He was born in Bishop's Waltham on 12th May 1887, the fifth of the seven known children of George Andrew Mears and Sarah Jane Mears. The 1891 Census shows him living with his parents and five siblings at Myrtle Cottage, Winchester Road. His father was then a solicitors' clerk. By 1901, the family (now with one more child) is still living in Winchester Road and Walter is shown as 12 but unusually, given his age, has an occupation as "post office telegraph messenger". The next Census in 1911 reveals that Walter is no longer living with his parents, who have moved to Waltham Chase, near Bishop's Waltham. He is, however, shown in that Census, as a gunner in the Royal Marine Artillery and a member of the crew of the battleship HMS *Swiftsure*, anchored in the Grand Harbour, Malta.

In 1913 Walter married Diana Jones and the couple moved into Valetta Cottage, Waltham Chase. Walter continued in the Navy but was killed at the battle of Jutland on 31st May 1916, aged 29, when HMS *Lion* was severely damaged, but not sunk. It is really very odd that Walter's name was omitted from the Memorial, particularly as his father, George Andrew Mears, is shown on the 1911 census as clerk to the Rural District Council.

George William NEWLAND (1892-1917)
Twice-wounded sergeant in the Rifle Brigade

George enlisted as Private No.S/964 in the 12th (Service) Battalion of the Rifle Brigade at Blackdown, on 4th September 1914. He was described at that time as 23 years old, 5' 9" tall, weighing just under ten stone, and having a fair complexion, blue eyes and light brown hair. A great many of the British Army service records relating to the Great War were lost or damaged by bombing in WWII but George's papers, although damaged and faded, are mostly readable and give a reasonably accurate time line for his service in the Rifle Brigade.

It seems he enrolled for a second time on 12th February 1915 and was sent to France with his Battalion on 21st July, where he was wounded on 25th September that year. He was sent back to England on 2nd October and admitted to hospital in London two days later, where he stayed for ten days. A month later he was sent back to France, but was admitted to hospital in Étaples with psoriasis on 21st November 1915.

He was promoted to lance corporal in September 1916 but was wounded again a month later. However he was able to rejoin his Battalion on 16th November 1916. He was promoted to corporal in January 1917 and then to sergeant in June, but was killed in action two months later on 18th August 1917, aged 25.

The War Diaries for the 12th Rifle Brigade show that at the date of George's death his Battalion was involved in the Battle of Langemarck (one of the initial phases of the Third Battle of Ypres, which itself was also known as Passchendaele), and his name heads a typed list included in the Diary of 32 casualties among the Other Ranks. In addition to the usual Victory and Service Medals, George was entitled to the 1915 Star.

George had been born in 1892 in Portsmouth to Henry Charles Newland and Elizabeth Newland (née Hayden). The 1901 Census shows all five of the Newland children (including George, then aged 9) with their grandparents in Shirrell Heath. This may have been for one day or for a longer period – the census requires only that all persons at the address on the night in question be recorded. The next census, in 1911, indicates that George (aged 19) is again with his parents, and is described as a "farmer's son, working on farm", at Dean, Bishop's Waltham.

Archibald Stanley PAICE (1882-1917)
Brewer's son died of wounds
Archibald was born in Bishop's Waltham in 1882, the son of Henry Richard Paice (a brewer), and Emily Paice (née Parker). The 1891 Census shows him (aged 9) living with his parents and siblings at Brewery House. Ten years later, in 1901, his parents and three of his siblings are living at The Elms, Bishop's Waltham, but the 19 year old Archibald is a chemist's apprentice, boarding at the same address as his elder brother, Howard – 84 Broad Street, Reading. Henry Paice, Archibald's father, died on 30th November 1903. The 1911 Census shows his mother, Emily, still living at The Elms.

In 1908 he married Bessie Jane Moody, at Steyning, Sussex, and by 1911 the young couple were living at 1 Tamar Cottages, Yiewsley, Middlesex, with

THE SERVICEMEN FROM BISHOP'S WALTHAM WHO DIED IN THE GREAT WAR

their son, Stanley Archibald, aged 1. But the Great War intervened. Archibald Paice enlisted, at Uxbridge, as Private No.G/13378, in the 1st Battalion of the East Kent Regiment (the Buffs). He died of wounds, aged 36, at the 3rd Military Hospital in Oxford on 13th December 1917, and is buried at the Hillingdon and Uxbridge Cemetery. His effects were sent to his widow, Bessie.

The 1st Battalion of the Buffs' War Diaries for November 1917 describe a movement to the front, and an intelligence summary for that time says: "Battalion marched to witness tank demonstrations. Six tanks took part and gave the Battalion some little idea as to the method proposed for the tank attacks in the forthcoming "Push"."

The Push in question was the start of the Battle of Cambrai. This was a massive British attack by artillery, infantry and tanks on 20th November 1917. By December each side had suffered about 40,000 men killed, wounded or missing, to no advantage. Although it is not certain, it seems likely that Archibald suffered his ultimately fatal wounds in this action.

Station Road circa 1908. The Elms, where the Paice family lived, was on the left behind the trees

Jack Benjamin PRICE (1893-1917)
Gamekeeper who died on the Western Front

The inscription on the War Memorial itself reads "P. Price". The name on the printed programme for the War Memorial dedication ceremony says "Philip Price", but the Christian name was amended, in pencil, presumably by one of the War Memorial Committee members, to read "Jack".

The FreeBMD index also records that the death of Jack's younger brother, Philip Albert Price, was registered in Southampton in 1985. So it seems that there was an error on the list used for the inscriptions on the War Memorial, and that probably (but not certainly) the person who should be remembered is not Philip but Jack Benjamin Price. The following is based on that premise.

Jack Price was born in Camberley in 1893 to John Edwin Price (a publican) and Ellen Price. The 1901 Census shows him, aged 8, living with his parents and younger brother, Philip Albert Price, at the Hop Poles, Mount Pleasant Road, Alton. By 1911 the family had moved to Dundridge, where John Edwin Price kept the Jubilee Tavern (now called The Hampshire Bowman). Jack is shown as aged 18 and a gamekeeper, his brother (now with an additional name) Philip Jubilee Albert as 13, and a new sibling, Gordon Edward, as aged 1.

The Index of UK Soldiers Died in the Great War lists John Benjamin Price (Jack being an alternative for John), born in Camberley, a Gunner in the Royal Horse and Field Artillery, No.109833 who enlisted at Winchester, as having died of wounds on 14th July 1917, aged 24. He is buried at the Loos Memorial, Loos-en-Gohelle, Nord-Pas-de-Calais, France.

Walter PRICE (1890? -1915)
Little is known of this man

Walter Price was born in Blackwater, Hampshire, in about 1890. He spent some time in Dundridge and enlisted in Bishop's Waltham in the 1st

Battalion of the Hampshire Regiment as Private No.8049, possibly in 1914. He was killed in action in France on 26th April 1915, aged about 25, and was entitled to the 1914 Star, in addition to the usual Service and Victory Medals. Unusually his Medals Card is marked to show that all medals were "returned" – perhaps no relatives could be identified, or none were then living. Walter's low regimental number might indicate an enlistment date closer to 1908.

The Hampshire's 1st Battalion was involved in particularly heavy fighting on the date of Walter's death and the following days, as is shown by the report in the regimental War Diary by their commanding officer, Lieutenant Colonel F.R. Hicks. This document, which was typed and presumably written with due consideration after the battle, refers to the battalion being at the head of the Ypres salient which was commanded by German artillery on ridges to the north and east: "these guns could be laid with deadly accuracy. For eight days and nights their guns never ceased. At times shells were falling on our trenches at the rate of about 50 a minute." He goes on to say, "we hung on from daylight on 26th until darkness on 3rd and not only did we not give a yard, but we pushed our trenches forward," and mentions that "the 26th was our worst day".

Although very little information has been found for Walter – no birth or census records, nor any war grave entries – it is interesting to note that in 1911 the publican of the Jubilee Tavern at Dundridge (now called The Hampshire Bowman) was John Edwin Price (see above). None of the publican's own sons were named Walter, but it may be that "our" Walter was a distant relative who had stayed, or perhaps worked at the Tavern, so accounting for his residence at Dundridge. There are several records of individuals named Walter Price returning from Canada and Australia in the run up to the start of WWI, but none is specifically identifiable – Walter Price is not an uncommon name.

Albert Edward PURNELL (1898-1918)
Caught up in the German 1918 Spring Offensive

Charles Purnell married Alice Goodwin 1890, their union being registered at Woolwich, Kent, the area in which both had been born[2]. In 1901 (when, in error, the Ancestry transcription of the Census lists the family under Parnell rather than Purnell) Charles and Alice were living in Congo Road, Plumstead, and had four children, all born in Plumstead, and all male: Charles aged 9; William 7; Arthur 5; and Albert 2. By 1911 they have moved. The census confirms that they have four boys, names the youngest as Albert Edward, then aged 12, and shows their address as 11 Clayland Cottages, Bishop's Waltham[3]. It also shows the occupation of Charles as that of a self-employed "jobbing gardener", although while at Plumstead, he had been working as an "engineer/turner". It may be that his change of domicile and occupation are connected. However, there are enough similarities between ages and places of birth given on both censuses for it to be reasonable to assume that the same family is being described.

Albert enlisted as Private No.30172 in the 4th Battalion of the Hampshire Regiment in October 1916, and was drafted to France in December. He was subsequently transferred as Private No.117967 to the 30th Machine Gun Corps. On 21st March 1918, with some 50 divisions having been released from the Eastern Front by the Russian surrender, the German Army launched Operation Michael, the first phase of their 1918 Spring Offensive, in the Somme area. At this time the 30th Machine Gun Corps was stationed near St Quentin. Their War Diary relates that the morning of 21st March was very misty – an intensive enemy bombardment (including many gas shells) started at 4.40am, followed at 8.00am by an overwhelming infantry attacked by crack troops, forcing a British retreat. It was not until 5th April, when, having failed to capture either Amiens or Arras, and facing increasingly strongly entrenched British units, the German commander, Eric Ludendorff, called off Operation Michael. It was during this period that Albert went missing.

---

[2] Although now part of Greater London, Woolwich was part of north Kent until 1889
[3] The National Roll of the Great War and the Commonwealth War Graves Records both give the address as "11 Claylands Road", but as Charles Purnell will have filled in his own details on the 1911 Census, it is likely that the correct address is 11 Claylands Cottages.

THE SERVICEMEN FROM BISHOP'S WALTHAM WHO DIED IN THE GREAT WAR

The Register of Soldiers' Effects shows that it was accepted for official purposes that his death took place on 29th March 1918. He was 20. He is remembered on the Pozières Memorial, Department de la Somme, Picardie, France. The entry in the UK, Commonwealth War Graves register records that Albert (No.117967) was the son of Charles and Alice Purnell, of 11 Claylands Road, Bishop's Waltham.

Esau RICHARDS (1899-1918)
A twin who died less than a month before the Armistice
Arthur Richards and Kate Whittenham were married in 1883. The previous census (1881) showed Kate as a parlour maid to Charles and Jessie Gunner at Brook House, Brook Street, while Arthur was a jeweller and watchmaker, living in Bank Street. By 1911 the Richards family had moved to the High Street, where Arthur also kept his jewellery shop. The family had increased considerably but not without some heart-break: eleven children had been born, of whom only eight were still living at the time of the Census. Among the eight were Queenie and Esau, twins born in 1899.

High Street circa 1917, with Arthur Richards' Jewllery shop under the nearest clock.

Esau Richards joined the 2nd Battalion of the Devon Regiment as Private No.70159, probably in 1917, but was subsequently transferred to the 8th (Service) Battalion of the Gloucestershire Regiment, as Private No.44558. He died on 21st October 1918 of wounds sustained in France/Flanders. He was 20. The War Diary of the 8th Battalion describes a successful attack on 20th October, in which high ground was taken to the north-east of the River Selle. It may be that Esau was fatally wounded in that action. He is buried at the Delsaux Farm Cemetery, Beugny, Nord-Pas-de-Calais, France. His effects were sent to his father, Arthur Richards. Esau's twin sister, Queenie, married James Robson Darnell, a farmer from Odiham, on 29th September 1923. A son, Francis James Robson Darnell, was born to them in 1924, and a daughter, Georgina Helen, in 1929. Queenie herself died at Winchester Hospital on 8th April 1959.

George Solomon RICHARDS (1879-1918)
A Royal Engineer buried in Gibraltar

Henry Solomon Richards and Annie Ford were married at St Mary's Portsea on 19th May 1872. Their third child, George, was born in the latter part of 1879. Both the 1891 and the 1901 Censuses show George living with his parents and siblings in the High Street, Bishop's Waltham. George's occupation is given initially as "scholar" and subsequently as "plumber". By 1911 the family had moved to Winchester Road, Bishop's Waltham, but George was no longer with them.

The military section of the 1911 Census records a George Richards (Royal Engineer, age 31, plumber, born about 1880 at Bishop's Waltham) as part of the military establishment under the command of Major General Sir Henry Jenner Scobell, at The Cape of Good Hope, South Africa. It is persuasive that George Richards has disappeared from the UK 1911 Census, and a George Richards of the right age, birthplace and occupation has appeared in South Africa, although not conclusive.

George's British Army service records are among those lost in WWII, however the Medal Index Card for George Richards, Royal Engineers,

Sapper No.8781 shows that he was entitled to the 1915 Star as well as the Service and Victory medals, and that he entered the Western European theatre of war on 29th June 1915. The War Graves Records relate that Sapper G.S. Richards, No.8781, Royal Engineers, son of Annie Richards and the late Henry Solomon Richards, of Winchester Road, Bishop's Waltham, died, aged 39, on 8th November 1918, just a few days before the end of the War. He was buried in Gibraltar's North Front Cemetery.

It is not clear how George Richards, who might have been serving in the Royal Engineers in South Africa pre-war, came first to France in 1915 and then to Gibraltar in 1918. The cemetery in Gibraltar was used throughout WWI for the burial of servicemen who died on ships calling at that port.

George's younger brother, William Henry Richards (see over), predeceased him, having died of wounds sustained at the Western Front some 15 months earlier.

Winchester Road, where George and William Richards lived

William Henry RICHARDS (1894-1917)
From Bishop's Waltham to Suez to the Somme

William Richards was born in Bishop's Waltham in 1894 to Henry Solomon Richards, an ironmonger and plumber, and Annie Richards (née Ford). The 1901 Census shows him, aged 7, living with his parents and siblings, including his older brother George (see above), in Winchester Road. Ten years later the next Census records that William is still with his parents and is working as an apprentice plumber under his father.

William's Army Service Records reveal that he enlisted in the 86th Field Company of the Royal Engineers, as Sapper No.69907, on 13th March 1915. His Medal Card shows that he was sent to Egypt on 19th July 1915. His unit, the 86th Field Company, was involved there for almost a year in the defence of the Suez Canal, but in June 1916 the 86th was ordered to France to reinforce the Third Army. It seems probable that they were sent from Alexandria to Marseilles in the SS *Megantic*, a White Star liner commandeered as a troopship in 1914. By 27th July 1916 they were in the front line on the Somme.

William enjoyed a ten day leave in England in January 1917 but when he returned to France he was very severely wounded on 8th August. He died in the Liverpool Merchants Mobile Hospital at Étaples two weeks later, on 22nd August 1917. He was 23. The hospital (also known as No.6 Hospital British Red Cross) was funded by the Liverpool Chamber of Commerce and staffed by volunteers from that City. William Richards is buried at the Étaples Military Cemetery, Nord-Pas-de-Calais, France; he was entitled to the 1915 Star, in addition to the usual Service and Victory Medals.

His personal effects were sent to his father, Henry Solomon Richards. Besides the usual toilet items they included: religious books, pocket book in leather case, 3 keys on ring, 2 stamps, goggles in case, photo case, writing pad, French book, writing pad, cigarette holder, cigarette case metal, 9ct. gold ring, discs, letters, photos, coins, cards, knife, scissors, watch case and strap. In a sad human touch, his father wrote, in November 1917, under his receipt for the effects: "Poor Will, I hope he is at rest."

THE SERVICEMEN FROM BISHOP'S WALTHAM WHO DIED IN THE GREAT WAR

Two of the items seem a little odd, but the goggles were probably intended for extra protection against gas, and the discs additional identity aids.

George and William's father, Henry Solomon Richards, was spared the trauma and pain of knowing that he'd lost a second son, as he died between July and September 1918, at the age of 71.

William Henry Richards (right) with friend and trophy
Pickelhaube (German officer's spiked helmet)

Arthur Follett SIMS/Thomas GREGORY (1883-1916)
Mysterious name change
Arthur Follett Sims, the first son of Ebenezer Sims and Elizabeth Sims (née Follett) was born on 5th September 1883 and baptised on 25th November in

that year at St Peter's Church in Bishop's Waltham. His father was for many years the schoolmaster of the Bishop's Waltham Board School. The 1911 Census shows that Ebenezer and Elizabeth had nine children, of whom eight were still living at that date. It is interesting to note that the middle name of each and every one of the Sims' children (both male and female) was Follett.

Arthur is recorded by the 1891 Census, aged 7, living at The School House in Bishop's Waltham with his parents and siblings, but he does not appear on either the 1901 or 1911 Censuses. It seems he left home early in life. There is an entry in the National Archives for the Royal Marines showing that Arthur Follett Sims joined the force at age 18 in 1901, but that his discharge was purchased in 1902. Another entry, in the Royal Navy Register of Seamen's Services, records that he served briefly (from 1st October 1905 to 17th May 1906) on HMS *Terrible* – seemingly as a trainee cook or steward – but that, despite having a "VG character", he was "discharged to shore – unsuitable".

The next available record puts Arthur in Canada where, in September 1914, he joined the 4th Battalion of the 1st Central Ontario Regiment of the Canadian Expeditionary Force, under the assumed name of Thomas Gregory, Private No.20621. This unit left Canada on 23rd September 1914 on the SS *Tyrolla* and reached England on 14th October, where the men underwent training at Lavington, before crossing the Channel on the SS *Atlantean* to St Nazaire, and moving up to the Western Front in February 1915.

Thomas Gregory (Arthur Sims) was killed in action, aged 33, on 8th October 1916 at Courcelette, during the prolonged battle of the Somme. The Canadian War Graves Register records that he is buried at the Vimy Memorial, and also reveals his real name, and shows that particulars of his death were sent to his father at The School House, Bishop's Waltham.

It may be that disappointment at the early failure to pursue his chosen naval or military career was the cause for Arthur's emigration and name change, but we shall probably never know. Neither will we know why he chose the name Thomas Gregory. At least two Thomas Gregorys lived in Bishop's

Waltham during the 1600 and 1700s – he may have picked the name from a tombstone but this is speculation.

His younger brother, Oswald, was killed in action in France three months later (see below).

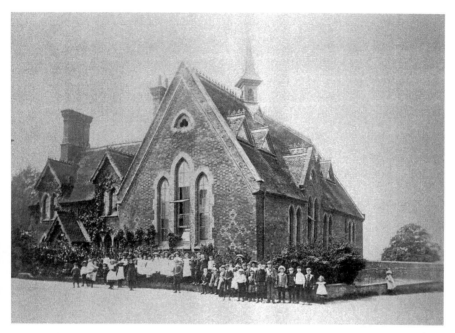

The School in Victoria Road with The School House, where the Sims family lived, on the left

Oswald Follett SIMS (1897-1917)
Schoolmaster's son killed in a quiet period
Oswald was born in the final quarter of 1897, at Bishop's Waltham, the fifth son of Ebenezer and Elizabeth Sims. In both the 1901 and 1911 Censuses he is shown living with his parents and siblings at the School House, Bishop's Waltham, although his older brother, Arthur, had already left home by then.

It was probably in 1916 that he joined the 1st Battalion of the Hampshire Regiment as Private No.24644 and was sent to France after basic training.

Oswald died from wounds on 22nd January 1917 and is buried at The Grove Town Cemetery, Méaulte, Picardie, France. He was 19. The Battalion's War Diary for January reports fine frosty weather, with snow on the ground, and comments on the difficulties of bringing up supplies. Casualties for the month were comparatively light: "Killed: 2 other ranks, wounded: 3 other ranks and Second Lieut. E.F. Jacob." It seems Oswald was unfortunate enough to have met his death during a very quiet period at the Front.

Within a few short months, Ebenezer and Elizabeth Sims had lost two of their sons.

Charles Henry SMITH (1892-1914)
From India to the Middle East
Researching 'Charles Smith' was bound to be difficult. The Ancestry website initially offers 63,327 possibilities! Choosing just one of them presents its problems.

The name on the War Memorial itself is "C. Smith" and the same is true of the Roll of Honour on the wall of St Peter's Church, but the printed programme for the dedication service is a little more forthcoming, saying "Charles Smith … 1st Dorset Regiment"

A plausible candidate for commemoration on the Bishop's Waltham War Memorial is Charles Henry Smith, born in 1892 in Droxford to William Henry and Alice Smith. The 1901 Census shows Charles, aged 8, living with his parents and three siblings (William, Albert and Rose) at Lower Farm Cottage in Exton. By 1911 it seems that Charles Henry had left the nest to go out to work (as a farm labourer) and was boarding with Ann Trimbee, a 59 year old widow who lived in Curdridge Lane, Bishop's Waltham. His father had also moved, to Dean, with his younger son, while his mother was lodging in Droxford.

Charles enlisted with the 2nd Battalion of the Dorsetshire Regiment as Private No.9157, at Gosport, probably before the war began. The 2nd Battalion of the Dorsetshire Regiment was in India at the outbreak of war and formed part of the Indian Expeditionary Force D which landed near Fao, in the Persian Gulf, on 6th November 1914, at the outset of the Mesopotamian Campaign. After taking Fao, the British and Indian troops advanced towards Basra, defeating the Ottomans at Sahil and occupying Basra itself on 21st November. Charles's Medal Index Card shows that he was a member of the Expeditionary Force, and that he was killed in action on 17th November during the advance. He was 22. The Register of Soldiers' Effects contains references to Poona, Sahil, and the Indian Army Expeditionary Force, and also records that Charles's effects were sent to his father, William Henry Smith. He is buried at the Basra War Cemetery, and the records there confirm that he was the son of William Henry and Alice Smith of Droxford.

William Charles STEELE (1886-1915)
Killed in action at Gallipoli

William, Private No.15239 of the 2nd Battalion of the Hampshire Regiment, was killed in action at Gallipoli, aged 29, on 29th June 1915. The 2nd Battalion had landed at Gallipoli, in the Cape Helles area, on 25th April 1915, and took part in heavy fighting near the village of Krithia, suffering many casualties from both combat and disease, before being evacuated to Alexandria in 1916.

Another man listed on our War Memorial, Leonard CONDUCT, also served in the 2nd Battalion of the Hampshires. He was killed at Gallipoli a few weeks later, on 2nd August 1915. It is not known whether the two knew one another.

William was born in Droxford in 1886, the third son of David and Mary Steele (née Goater). His elder brothers were George and Alfred, and he also had a younger sister, Emily. His father David died young, at 31, in 1888, and his mother was remarried in 1896 to William Frank Linney. The 1901 Census shows William living in his stepfather's household, but by 1911 he had apparently moved out and was recorded as a visitor in the house occupied by George Tilbury and his daughter, Lily, in Bank Street, Bishop's Waltham. William and Lily were married in 1913. A child named Jack Steele was born to a mother whose maiden name was Tilbury in about December 1915, but unfortunately died at birth or soon after. It is possible, even likely, that this baby was the son of William and Lily, and, if so, the mother must have been doubly stricken to lose both husband and son in the same year.

Bank Street, where William Steele was staying with the Tilbury family, circa 1912

Frank Austin STUBBS (1890-1918)
Probably a victim of Spanish 'Flu

Frank Austin Stubbs, Acting Sergeant No.GS/72421 in the 17th Battalion of the Royal Fusiliers (City of London) Regiment, died of influenza, aged 28, in France, on 14th November 1918. He is buried at the Terlincthum British Cemetery, Nord-Pas-de-Calais, France. His effects were sent to his father, Frank Stubbs.

Frank Austin Stubbs was born in Bishop's Waltham in 1890, the first child of Frank Stubbs (auctioneer) and Louisa Catherine Stubbs (née Bond). The 1891 Census shows him living with his parents in The Folly House, Free Street. By 1901 Frank had moved with the family, which now consisted of four children and their parents, to Trellingham Farm Cottages. (This could well be Trullingham Farm, Wintershill, between Bishop's Waltham and Durley.) The 1911 Census reports him, aged 20, working as a "clerk to auctioneer" and living in the family house, Wolversdene in Bishop's Waltham.

It has not been possible to find Frank's Army Service Records, and it is not known when he joined up, nor why he enlisted in the Royal Fusiliers instead of the local regiment, but his medal records show that he went to France on 18th January 1918, and that he is entitled to the Service and Victory medals.

Francis WATSON (1882-1917)
A Highlander from Bishop's Waltham

Francis Watson was born in Scrayingham, Yorkshire, to John F. Watson (a gardener) and Sarah Ann Watson (née Green, a sub-postmistress). The 1891 Census shows him living there, aged 9, with his parents and three siblings.

His marriage to Blanche Emily New, a Bishop's Waltham girl, was registered at Droxford in the third quarter of 1909, and the 1911 Census reveals them living with their 1 year old daughter, Kathleen Lucy, at Gilbert's Knapp, Beeches Hill, Bishop's Waltham, Blanche's father's house. They went on to have two more children, Alice Sophia (born 1912) and Reginald Walter (born 1918). Blanche herself lived on until 16th July 1959 and is buried in St Peter's Churchyard. Her gravestone (presumably erected by her daughters) also refers to Reginald Walter, who was killed in 1941 during WWII, when the SS *Sparta*, a small collier, struck a mine off Dungeness, and sank with the loss of her entire crew of nine.

Francis may have joined the Territorials before leaving Yorkshire, or may have had some family connection with Scotland, because he is shown by the Register of UK Soldiers Killed in the Great War to have enlisted (probably in 1916) at Winchester, in the 7th Blythswood Territorial Battalion of the Highland Light Infantry (HLI). Blythswood is a suburb of Glasgow.

Earlier in the War, the 1/5th and the 1/7th Battalions of the HLI moved together and on 26th May 1915 had sailed from Devonport to Egypt, and then on to Gallipoli, landing at Cape Helles on 3rd July 1915. At the end of the Gallipoli operation, in January 1916, they were evacuated to Egypt and were employed in the defence of the Suez Canal and in the Palestine Campaign, until being sent to the Western Front in 1918.

It seems likely that Francis Watson was one of a contingent deployed to reinforce the HLI in Egypt. The route with least exposure to U-boat attack would have been to cross the Channel into France, to move south to the Mediterranean coast, and then to take ship for Alexandria. This "safe" course was probably being followed by Francis's contingent, but nevertheless he was drowned on 4th May 1917, aged 35, when the 14,000-ton troopship SS *Transylvania*, despite being escorted by two Japanese destroyers, was torpedoed by the German submarine U-63, commanded by Otto Schultze, some two and a half miles off the town of Savona, in the Bay of Genoa. The ship, which was carrying a full load of soldiers and some 60 nurses from Marseilles to Egypt, did not sink immediately. One of the destroyers (the *Matsu*) came alongside to take off the passengers, while the other (the *Sakaki*) circled to prevent the U-boat surfacing. About half an hour later the submarine fired a second torpedo. The *Matsu* reversed engines and saved herself but the *Transylvania* was hit for a second time. One report says that she sank immediately after the second torpedo but another, by Lt. Philip Murphy RAMC (who was one of the passengers), declares that she stayed afloat for another one and a half hours, and indeed that seems more likely. Of the approximately 3,400 people aboard some 3,000 were saved, but ten crew members and some 400 soldiers were lost. Small vessels came out from the Italian coastal fishing villages to supplement the efforts of the destroyers and the *Transylvania*'s own lifeboats – Lt. Murphy himself was picked up by a tug from Savona. Many casualties of the disaster were buried in the Savona Town Cemetery, Liguria, Italy – Francis Watson was one of them.

The Japanese destroyer *Sakaki* was herself torpedoed about a month later, off the coast of Crete. Although the ship survived and was repaired, 68 of her crew were killed. Both Italy and Japan were on the side of the Allies in WWI (see Background to the Great War).

THE SERVICEMEN FROM BISHOP'S WALTHAM WHO DIED IN THE GREAT WAR

Reginald Frank WEAVIL (1898-1917)
Died near the River Piave in Italy

Reginald Weavil was born in the last quarter of 1898, in Bishop's Waltham, to Alfred Weavil and Louisa Weavil (née Barnes). The 1901 Census records him, aged 2, living with his parents and siblings in Ladysmith Terrace. Ten years later, in 1911, he is shown as a 12 year old schoolboy living with his family in Albany Terrace, Newtown, Bishop's Waltham.

Reginald enlisted in Winchester (probably in early 1917) as Private No.25730, in the 15th Service Battalion of the Hampshire Regiment. In September 1917 this unit was amalgamated with the dismounted 1/1st Hampshire Yeomanry, and in November the combined force was moved from France to Italy to help stiffen Italian resistance in the Treviso area. Reginald Frank was killed in action on 11th December 1917 and is buried at the Giavera British Cemetery, Giavera del Montello, Provincia di Treviso, Veneto, Italy. He was 19. His effects were sent to his mother, Louisa Weavil.

Edwin WEEKS (1896-1915)
Died of enteric fever in Egypt

Edwin Weeks was born in 1896 in Kilmeston, near Alresford, to Joseph Weeks and Ellen Margaret Weeks (née Dillow). In 1901, with Edwin then 5 years of age, the family was still living in Kilmeston. The 1911 Census shows him working as a "domestic groom", and living with his parents and six of his 10 siblings, at Beauworth.

In September 1914 Edwin volunteered for the 15th (The King's) Hussars, but subsequently he was transferred to the 7th (Service) Battalion of the Gloucester Regiment, as Private No.22438. In June 1915 the Battalion sailed from Avonmouth, landing at Gallipoli the following month. Edwin apparently became ill and was evacuated to Eygpt. He died of "enteric fever" (typhoid) on 10th October 1915 in the General Hospital at Alexandria, Egypt. He was 19.

Edwin is commemorated on the Chatby Military War Memorial in Alexandria, as well as on the Bishop's Waltham Memorial. He was initially granted only the General Service and Victory Medals, but the Medal Roll Index Cards show that he was also awarded the 1914-15 Star, after the intervention of his mother, who was then living in Basingwell Street, Bishop's Waltham. The National Roll of the Great War also gives his address as Basingwell Street.

Edwin's older brother, Wilfred, was killed in action on the Western Front exactly two years later.

Basingwell Street, where Edwin and Wilfred Weeks lived, circa 1905

Wilfred Joseph WEEKS (1891-1917)
Stable lad killed on the Western Front

Joseph Weeks and Ellen Margaret Dillow married in the second quarter of 1888, their union being recorded at the Droxford Registry Office. The 1911 Census shows that they had 11 children, all of whom were then still living. Wilfred, their third child, was born in 1891 and baptized, a little belatedly, in Kilmeston on 1st May 1892. Both the Births and Christening Records show his Christian names as Wilfred Joseph, but there seems to have been indecision as to which of his Christian names to use in the Censuses – he is Joseph in 1891, Wilfred in 1901, and Joseph again in 1911, at which time he was a "stable lad" working in Upper Chilcombe. For his Army service he seems to have settled for Joseph.

Wilfred (Joseph) enlisted in the Wiltshire Regiment in January 1917 as Private No. 31740, but was subsequently transferred to the 8th (Service) Battalion of the Devonshire Regiment as Private No. 30708. After training he was drafted to the Western Front, where he was killed in action, probably during the 3rd Battle of Ypres, on 2nd October 1917, aged 26. He is commemorated on the Tyne Cot Memorial, Zonnebeke, Ypres, West Flanders, Belgium. His effects were sent to his father, Joseph Weeks.

The Weeks family lived in the Alresford, Exton, Kilmeston and Beauworth areas from 1888 to 1911, but seemingly moved to Bishop's Waltham at some time after 1911. There is clear evidence that Ellen Weeks applied to the War Office for the award of the 1914 Star to Edwin, Wildred's younger brother, and also gave information to the National Roll of the Great War about both Wilfred and Edwin (and also about Sydney, their younger brother, who survived the war) from an address in Basingwell Street, Bishop's Waltham.

Wilfred's younger brother, Edwin, had died of typhoid fever two years earlier, in 1915 (see above).

THEY DIED THAT WE MIGHT LIVE

Dulce et Decorum Est

Bent double, like old beggars under sacks,
Knock-kneed, coughing like hags, we cursed through sludge,
Till on the haunting flares we turned our backs,
And towards our distant rest began to trudge.
Men marched asleep. Many had lost their boots
But limped on, blood-shod. All went lame; all blind;
Drunk with fatigue; deaf even to the hoots
Of gas-shells dropping softly behind.

Wilfred Owen

Chapter 5

A STORYLINE OF THE GREAT WAR

The Great War was fought on many separate fronts between many different nations, and it was fought on land, sea and in the air. This chapter is a brief description of the battles and theatres of war in which these men from Bishop's Waltham served. It is intended to provide a wider context for their service and sacrifice.

1914

The Western Front

The opening phase of the war in Western Europe was the launch of an invasion of Belgium and France by the German Imperial Army. It has become known as the 'Battle of the Frontiers' as both sides attacked and counter-attacked across northern France and Belgium in a series of almost simultaneous battles at Mulhouse, Lorraine, the Ardennes, Charleroi, and Mons. At the Battle of the Marne (6-10th September) the initial German advance was first halted and then forced back.

Immediately the next phase began, known as the 'Race for the Sea'. This was an attempt by both sides to outflank their opponent to the north – all the way up to the Channel coast. On this, the Western Front, the only casualty from Bishop's Waltham in 1914 was Gunner Herbert GIBSON, who died of wounds near Merville on 28th November. It seems possible that he was wounded at the First Battle of Ypres (19th October-22nd November), part of the 'Race for the Sea'.

Herbert Gibson was one of the "Old Contemptibles", a term given to those soldiers of the British Expeditionary Force who served within range of German field artillery between 5th August and 22nd November 1914. So named because of a supposed Order of the Day issued by the Kaiser which referred to the British Force as "Sir John French's contemptible little army". No such order has ever been found, but this small professional army defended Ypres despite being outnumbered by a German army ten times their size. In so doing, they stopped the Germans reaching the critical Channel ports like Dunkirk. There is a memorial to the Old Contemptibles in Westminster Abbey.

Back in Britain on the following day, 29th November, Gunner George CASEY died of a cerebral abscess in hospital at Portsmouth.

Mesopotamia

Elsewhere, another challenge for Britain was that on 4th August 1914, the same day that Britain declared war, Turkey (the Ottoman Empire) signed a secret treaty with Germany. Nearly three months later, on 29th October 1914, Turkey opened hostilities against Russia.

From Britain's point of view, Turkey's entry into the war posed three new threats: to the British colonies in the Gulf of Aden and the Persian Gulf, to the Suez Canal (a vital link with all the eastern parts of the British Empire), and to the critical source of oil in Mesopotamia (modern-day Iraq).

In 1913 Winston Churchill, First Lord of the Admiralty, had signed an exclusive contract with the Anglo-Persian Oil Company (later BP) to provide oil for the British Navy. This was part of a major modernisation plan designed to move the navy from coal-fired to oil-fired engine rooms. The Anglo-Persian Oil Company's oil fields in Mesopotamia were within the Ottoman Empire and therefore needed to be urgently secured.

On 6th November 1914, British offensive action began with the naval bombardment of the point where the Shatt-al-Arab (river) meets the Persian Gulf. This was followed by the landing of the British Indian Expeditionary Force D, comprising the 6th (Poona) Division. Once landed they marched to take Basra.

Here Private Charles SMITH was killed in action on 17th November in the battle for Basra, which was occupied five days later.

The Navy
Although right from the start the Royal Navy was engaged in operations around the world, the tragic explosion that destroyed the battleship HMS *Bulwark* occurred much closer to home, in Sheerness Harbour, Kent. Sub-lieutenant Edward GUNNER was killed in the explosion on 26th November.

Bishop's Waltham lost four of its servicemen in 1914.

1915

In February 1915 Gunner Thomas ANDREWS, serving in the Royal Artillery, died of pneumothorax (collapsed lung) while undergoing training in England.

Western Front
After the 'Race to the Sea', in 1915 the Western Front descended into a series of 'Battles for a Breakthrough' with attempts to dislodge the entrenched enemy opposite. The first in the British Sector was the Battle of Neuve Chapelle (10-13th March), launched to take the high ground and create a threat to the German Army occupying Lille. Although the British broke through the German Front Line and captured the village of Neuve Chapelle, the German Sixth Army carried out counter-attacks and the British were stopped from advancing any further. Private Ambrose BEST was killed in action during the battle.

In May 1915 the Allies carried out another combined offensive north of Arras towards Lille. This was the Second Battle of Artois (9th May-18th June). The aim was to push the Germans off the dominating high ground of the Loretto and Vimy Ridges north of Arras. By the end of the offensive there were approximately 100,000 French casualties, 26,000 British casualties and 90,000 German casualties. Captain William HEWETT was killed in action on the first day of the Battle of Aubers Ridge – a part of this wider battle. It is sobering to know that life expectancy in the trenches on the Western Front for junior officers was just six weeks. Expected to lead by example when attacking, they were prime targets for enemy sharpshooters and machine-gunners.

The Second Battle of Ypres (22nd April-25th May 1915) started on a pleasant spring afternoon with the full-scale trial of a new weapon: a cloud of poisonous chlorine gas released by the German Fourth Army, followed by an infantry attack. The German infantry's advance behind the cloud was rapid, the Allied Front Line was broken across a seven-mile front and the way to Ypres was open by the end of the day. Only a swift response from the 1st Canadian Division prevented a decisive breakthrough. The battle for the defence of Ypres and the recapture of lost ground included more German chlorine gas attacks against the Allied troops.

On the 26th April Private Walter PRICE was killed in action when the 1st Battalion of the Hampshire Regiment was exposed to German artillery on the Ypres salient as part of this battle.

On 15th May Rifleman Donald BRUCE died of wounds at St Omer. It is likely that he was injured during this battle for Ypres.

Major Andrew KING, an officer in the 7th Battalion of the Argyll and Sutherland Highlanders, was wounded by shrapnel on 24th May, during the Ypres battle, and died four days later.

Fighting continued around Ypres and Rifleman Alfred EMMETT was killed in action on the 31st July. On the 9th August Sapper William MATTHEWS, a professional soldier in the Royal Engineers, was listed missing, presumed dead.

The final casualty from Bishop's Waltham on the Western Front in 1915 was on 7th October, when Captain Benjamin GUNNER, who had received the Military Cross in June, was hit by a stray bullet, again near Ypres.

A STORYLINE OF THE GREAT WAR

Gallipoli

Winston Churchill, as First Lord of the Admiralty, conceived of a plan to force the Dardanelles (a strait only a mile wide at its narrowest point) and take Istanbul, thus knocking Turkey out of the war and opening supply routes to Britain's ally, Russia.

A force of 18 battleships (regarded as too old to face the modernised German Navy) and assorted cruisers and destroyers attempted to take the straits in early March 1915 but the channel was heavily mined and, after significant losses, the attempt was called off.

An alternative plan was devised to mount a land invasion of the straits and the Australian and New Zealand Army Corps (ANZAC), in training in Egypt before going on to France, were selected to form the core of the 78,000 troops, including British and French divisions, which were assembled to undertake the landings.

Unfortunately, a five-week delay, partly due to bad weather, meant that the Turkish 5th Army had time to prepare their defences. So when, on 25th April, landings began on six beaches around the peninsular, from the start the troops were subject to heavy fire from artillery, machine guns and rifles from the ridges above them. The British and French landed at Cape Helles, while the small cove where the Australians and New Zealanders landed, called Ari Burnu, became known as ANZAC Cove. More troops would land later at Suvla Bay.

Private Ralph BAILEY had immigrated to Australia and then subsequently joined the Australian Imperial Forces and landed on that first day. He was seriously wounded and died two days later.

By June, in the Cape Helles sector, both sides had become entrenched near the village of Krithia. The 2nd Battalion of the Hampshire Regiment (part of the 88th Brigade) was involved in the nearby Battle of Gully Ravine on 28th June and Private William STEELE was killed in action the following day. Just over a month later, on 6th August, Private Leonard CONDUCT, also serving in the 2nd Battalion, was killed in action, probably in the opening attack in the Battle of Krithia Vineyard that started that afternoon. British casualties in the first 24 hours of this fighting were just under 3,500.

On the 10th October, Private Edwin WEEKS, who had been evacuated from Gallipoli to Egypt with typhoid fever, died in hospital at Alexandria.

As autumn turned to winter, the Gallipoli campaign drifted and it was clear a stalemate had been reached. In October 1915 Bulgaria had joined the Central Powers and this opened up a direct line of communication between Germany and Istanbul – through Bulgaria. So German armaments, including heavy artillery and other supplies, now began arriving to help the Ottoman army.

In December the decision was taken to evacuate all Allied forces from the Gallipoli peninsula. This was carried out between 20th December and 9th January 1916. The British Army had suffered more than 120,000 casualties, including more than 34,000 killed. The Australian and New Zealand Corps suffered more than 35,500 casualties, including nearly 11,500 killed. ANZAC Day commemorations recognise the scale of this loss.

During 1915 Bishop's Waltham lost 13 of its servicemen.

1916

Conscription
Since the outbreak of war the British Government had relied on voluntary enlistment but by 1916 it was clear that it would be necessary to introduce conscription. The first Act came into force on 2nd March 1916. It specified that men from 18 to 41 years old were liable to be called up for service in the army, unless they were married, widowed with children, serving in the Royal Navy, a minister of religion, or working in one of a number of reserved occupations. A second Act in May 1916 extended liability for military service to married men and, later, a third Act in 1918 extended the upper age limit to 51.

The War at Sea

By 1916, the British were keeping a tight blockade on Germany which, given its short northern coastline, was not unduly difficult to enforce. Germany's High Seas Fleet had been commanded by Admiral von Poul but he was replaced by a new commander, Admiral Reinhardt von Scheer. Scheer was determined to break the blockade by forcing a battle with the British Navy. This battle, between the British Grand Fleet and the German High Seas Fleet off Denmark's Jutland peninsula, brought together the two most powerful naval forces of their time.

While land battles like Gallipoli, the Somme and Passchendaele are widely described, the sea battle of Jutland is perhaps less well known – so we have included a more detailed description written by Carl Graham, to provide a detailed account of what happened. Not least because five of the men killed in action came from Bishops Waltham – the largest number of our servicemen lost in such a single, short battle during the war.

The Battle of Jutland

The Battle of Jutland took place on 31st May 1916, the greatest sea battle that has been fought, and ever will be fought, solely between surface warships. Over 250 ships and 105,000 men were engaged in a running battle lasting 13 hours over hundreds of square miles of sea, which resulted in the loss of 25 ships and 8,645 men (including at least five men from Bishop's Waltham), and 1,181 wounded.

On the afternoon of 30th May 1916, the Admiralty informed Admiral Jellicoe, the Commander-in-Chief of the Grand Fleet, that some elements of the German High Seas Fleet were preparing to sail. The Grand Fleet subsequently sailed from Scapa Flow and Invergordon, while the Battlecruiser Fleet, under the command of Vice Admiral Sir David Beatty, sailed from Rosyth to rendezvous with the Grand Fleet near the Danish coast. At the same time, the German fleet was steaming north-west, heading for an eventual meeting with Jellicoe's battle squadrons.

WE WILL REMEMBER THEM

© Imperial War Museum Q68706

Part of the British Grand Fleet in the North Sea

British cruisers scouted ahead of the battle fleet, and on the afternoon of 31st May the cruisers HMS *Galatea* and *Phaeton* saw enemy warships on the horizon. *Galatea* fired the opening shots in what has become known as the Battle of Jutland. Beatty, thinking that only light German forces were ahead, went to cut off their line of retreat. The battleships of the 5th Battle Squadron and Beatty's battlecruisers became separated, with disastrous results. The British ships were lured into combat with the whole of the High Seas Fleet, which registered hits on HMS *Tiger*, *Lion* and *Princess Royal*. Beatty needed support, but the four battleships were eight miles away. When *Lion* was hit all men in the gun turret were killed or wounded; one of the dead was Gunner Walter MEARS.

At the rear of the British battlecruisers, HMS *Indefatigable* was hit by shells, one of which exploded a magazine, and the ship began to sink. Hit by another salvo the ship capsized and sank. All but three of *Indefatigable's* company of 1,017 officers and men were lost, including George LOVELL.

A STORYLINE OF THE GREAT WAR

Another Bishop's Waltham man, Edward BARFOOT, was on the battlecruiser HMS *Queen Mary*, manning one of the guns. The ship was hit by several shells, her magazines exploded, and she plunged to the bottom of the sea. All but 18 of her 1,266 men were lost, including Edward.

Admiral Hood's squadron of battlecruisers, led by HMS *Invincible*, hurried to give support to Beatty. When the parts of the Grand Fleet eventually merged and engaged with the German ships, the whole of the High Seas Fleet retreated. However, during the retreat *Invincible* was hit and torn apart by a huge explosion. Nearly all on board lost their lives, including Robin GIFFARD-BRINE and Admiral Hood (who lived in Upham). Also during the retreat of the High Seas Fleet, HMS *Princess Royal* was hit by shells, one of which destroyed X turret, killing Frederick ANDREWS. As visibility decreased, the German ships made their escape. Although further engagements took place, the chance of decisive action was over. The German fleet returned to harbour. Both sides claimed victory, but neither claim is valid. Although the German High Seas Fleet suffered fewer losses (11 ships sunk and just over 2,500 dead compared with 14 ships and over 6,000 dead), several surviving German ships were so badly damaged that they took months to repair. Admiral Jellicoe, on the other hand, reported 24 battleships ready for action the day after the battle.

Jutland will always take its place in history as the greatest sea battle ever fought between opposing fleets of battleships. When, toward the end of October 1918, in the closing days of the war, the German Admiralty under Admiral Scheer ordered the High Seas Fleet to sea again to fight the British Navy in one last gesture of defiance, the German sailors saw it as a suicide mission and mutinied. Their refusal to obey orders spread rapidly. By 4th November 1918 the sailors' revolt had turned into the revolution in Germany that swept the Kaiser from power. It remains open to debate as to whether the Royal Navy won or lost at Jutland, but this was one of the battles that eventually led to the successful conclusion of the war for Britain and her Allies, and in which the men whose names are commemorated on Bishop's Waltham's War Memorial played their part.

Western Front

With both sides now deeply entrenched on the Western Front, the Chief of the German General Staff, General Erich von Falkenhayn, doubted that a breakthrough was imminent. So he decided to "bleed France white" by inflicting unbearable casualties on the French army. He chose to launch a long drawn-out, large-scale offensive at Verdun — a fortress which the French would hold onto as a matter of national pride and because it guarded the route to Paris. German artillery was massed on a short front and the infantry offensive was launched by the German Fifth Army with one million men against a French force of about 200,000.

The Allies were concerned about France's ability to withstand the level of dead and wounded that ensued. It was therefore decided that the British Army would launch a planned offensive on the Somme to help relieve pressure on the French and to draw German reinforcements away from Verdun.

The battle began in the early morning of 1st July after an artillery bombardment lasting seven days — something not witnessed on any other battlefield before. The first day of the battle claimed over 58,000 British casualties, of whom more than 19,000 were killed. This is the largest loss on a single day in the history of the British Army. The first day of July 1916 was a day of tragedy for many thousands of families in Britain, including the Epps family, living in Free Street, whose only child, Private Louis EPPS, was amongst those killed on that day. Over a period of four and a half months the battle of the Somme continued in several phases, and continued to take many lives.

The first phase lasted from 1st-17th July and included the Battles of Albert, Bazentin Ridge and Fromelles. The second phase (14th July-15th September) included the Battles of Delville Wood, Pozières, Guillemont and Ginchy.

© Imperial War Museum Q3978

Battle of Bazentin Ridge. Troops of the Hampshire Regiment resting before going into the trenches in the early days of the Somme offensive July 1916.

It was during this second phase that, on 9th August, two corporals in the 2nd Battalion of the Hampshire Regiment, both from Bishop's Waltham, died in a surprise phosgene gas attack by the Germans. They were Corporal William MAY and Corporal Harry LACEY. On 3rd September, Private Charlie HAMMOND was also killed in action, possibly in the Battle of Guillemont (3rd-6th September).

The third and final phase of the Battle of the Somme (15th September-18th November) included the Battles of Flers-Courcelettes (when tanks were used for the very first time), Morval, Thiepval Ridge, Transloy Ridge, Ancre Heights and the Battle of Ancre.

WE WILL REMEMBER THEM

© Imperial War Museum Q 1568

Flooded area in the Ancre Valley toward the end of the Somme offensive, November 1916

On the 13th October Private William CONDUCT was killed, quite probably during the Battle of Transloy Ridge (1st October-11th November). Five days later, on 18th October, Private Arthur SIMS, who had immigrated to Canada and then later joined the 1st Central Ontario Regiment of the Canadian Expeditionary Force, died in fighting at Courcelettes.

The final death of a serviceman from Bishop's Waltham in 1916 was that of Corporal Frederick COOK. A member of a Royal Field Artillery mortar battery, he was killed in action on the day after Christmas.

In 1916 Bishop's Waltham lost a further 12 of its servicemen.

1917

On the 20th February, Private George COTTLE died of broncho-pneumonia at Woolwich Hospital in England.

Western Front
In August 1916 the German Chief of Staff, General Erich von Falkenhayn, had been dismissed and a dual command was put in place with Field Marshal von Hindenburg and General Ludendorff. They determined that the German armies should fall back to a new, heavily fortified line (the Hindenburg Line). On 17th February the Germans began this planned withdrawal.

But it was some days earlier, on the 22nd January, that the first casualty from Bishop's Waltham died in 1917. Private Oswald SIMS died of wounds – one of just two soldiers serving in the 1st Battalion of the Hampshire Regiment to die that month. His brother had died on the Somme the previous October.

The Allies had intended to go onto the offensive and this strategic withdrawal by the Germans created some dislocation to their plans. However the British Battle of Arras opened on 9th April and would continue for nearly a month.

Four days earlier, on the 5th April, Gunner William CUTLER – aged just 19 – was killed in action near Ypres.

On April 10th, Private Ernest LEE died of his wounds. These may have been inflicted during the First Battle of the Scarpe (9th-14th April) in which his Battalion was involved.

On 7th June 1917 the British Commander-in-Chief, General Haig, launched the first phase of an offensive which was intended to break out of the Ypres Salient. This was the Battle of Messines (7th-14th June). Gunner William FURSEY died of wounds on 19th June, probably received during this battle. On the 14th July, Gunner Jack PRICE also died of his wounds, though it is unclear where these were inflicted.

The next phase of the British Flanders offensive was the launch of the Third Battle of Ypres, also known as Passchendaele (31st July-6th November). The preliminary bombardment before the battle lasted for 10 days, during which time 3,000 guns fired more than four million artillery shells. However, shortly after the start of the battle rain began to fall and did not stop in the following weeks. This constant rain produced conditions totally unsuited to the movement of men, animals, artillery pieces or tanks. But the battle still ground on for months.

© Imperial War Museum Q 5935

Stretcher bearers struggle through deep mud to carry a wounded man to safety during the Third Battle of Ypres (Passchendaele), August 1917

In August 1917 three soldiers from Bishop's Waltham died. Sergeant George NEWLAND was killed in action on 18th August 1917, probably at the Battle of Langemarck (16th-18th August). On 22nd August Sapper William

RICHARDS, who had been severely wounded on 8th August, died in hospital. Then Private Francis HIGGINS was killed in action on 27th August, probably in this Third Battle of Ypres.

In October, as the Third Battle of Ypres ground on, Private Wilfred WEEKS was killed in action on 2nd October 1917, possibly at the Battle of Polygon Wood (26th September-3rd October).

The following month Private William GARSIDE was killed in action on 21st November – probably during the Battle of Cambrai (20th November – 7th December). Private Archibald PAICE died of wounds at the 3rd Military Hospital at Oxford on 13th December 1917. It seems possible that these wounds were also received at the Battle of Cambrai.

The War at Sea
Under Allied blockade, Germany relied on its submarines (U-boats) to damage Allied supply lines in an attempt to create its own blockade against Britain and France. For U-boats there were two routes to the Atlantic, the route around the north of Scotland or the faster route through the English Channel. The Royal Navy formed a Northern Patrol for the former and the Dover Patrol (based at Dover and Dunkirk) to cover the Channel.

On 8th February 1917, Stoker Charles BELL was serving on a destroyer, HMS *Ghurka*, as part of the Dover Patrol. It hit a mine off Dungeness and sank with a large loss of life, including his.

Some months later trainee telegraphist Edward Patrick GORE was serving on another Dover Patrol destroyer, HMS *Tartar*, on 17th June when it too hit a mine in the Channel. Nearly all hands were killed – including him.

On 11th December a British convoy left Lerwick in the Shetlands, bound for Bergen in Norway. It was attacked by German destroyers and Stoker Herbert HAMMOND was serving on one of the destroyer escorts – HMS *Partridge*.

Outgunned by the Germans, the ship was sunk and 97 crew members died, including Herbert.

Mesopotamia
Fighting in Mesopotamia had continued since 1914 and Corporal Neil GIBSON had fought there since he arrived on 18th March 1915. He died on Boxing Day 1917. Deaths from disease – such as cholera, typhoid and malaria – were very high in the Mesopotamian campaign.

The Salonika Front (Macedonian Campaign)
The spark that started the Great War was the shooting of Archduke Franz Ferdinand of Austria by a Bosnian-Serb. This led the Austro-Hungarian Empire, with the unconditional support of Germany, to declare war on Serbia in July 1914. Although the Austro-Hungarian army invaded Serbia on three occasions during 1914, contrary to expectations they were driven back each time.

Bulgaria, Serbia's neighbour, had the largest army in the Balkans and which side it chose would be critical. After being courted by both sides, Bulgaria finally joined the Central Powers with Germany and Austro-Hungary, and in October 1915 declared war on Serbia.

In the same month the Austro-Hungarian Balkan army, supported by the German 11th Army, made deep inroads into northern Serbia. Simultaneously two Bulgarian armies attacked Serbia from the west. Despite great courage and sacrifice, Serbia's army was forced south and faced imminent defeat. In the end it was ordered to retreat into Montenegro and then into Albania. Some 125,000 remaining Serbian troops reached the Adriatic coast and embarked on Italian transport ships bound for Corfu.

The Allies had finally sent a combined British and French force to help Serbia. They arrived in Thessalonica (Salonika) in Greece in September 1915, too late to make any significant difference, but it did open a new theatre of war for the British Army. What became known as the British Salonika Force fought alongside French, Serbian, Russian, Italian and Greek troops, and suffered more than 27,000 casualties in the Macedonian campaign.

Malaria (endemic in northern Greece at this time) and other diseases caused ten casualties for every one inflicted by the enemy. So it was that Private Albert EMMETT of Bishop's Waltham was taken ill and evacuated by ship to a hospital in Malta, where he died on 20th February 1917.

By March 1917 a multinational Allied force, under French General Maurice Sarrail, numbering 500,000 troops faced the Bulgarian Army as well as German, Austro-Hungarian and Turkish units, totalling 300,000 men. The British Salonika Force under General George Milne held 90 miles of front, including the key strategic position at Doiran (part of Serbia at that time).

Sarrail launched an offensive in April 1917, with French, Italian, Russian and Serbian troops. In support, the British attempted to capture Bulgarian positions around Doiran. When this offensive failed, static trench warfare continued until autumn 1918. It was here that Private Frederick HARVELL, serving with the Hampshire Regiment, died of his wounds on 17th April. He would probably have been wounded in the fighting that preceded the Battle of Doiran (22nd April-9th May).

The Italian Front

Although a member of the Triple Alliance when war broke out, Italy almost immediately declared itself neutral. After receiving secret promises from the Allies in the Treaty of London, Italy entered the war on 23rd May 1915 on the Allied side.

Italy had longstanding grievances with Austria-Hungary, dating back to the Congress of Vienna in 1815 after the Napoleonic Wars, which granted several regions of northern Italy to the Austrians. By entering the war they hoped to annex the Austrian Littoral and northern Dalmatia as well as the territories of Trentino and South Tyrol.

The Italian government hoped for a surprise offensive, but the Italian army still suffered equipment and munition shortages after the Italo-Turkish War in Libya (1911–1912). This allowed the Austro-Hungarian troops to occupy and fortify the high ground of the Julian Alps and Karst Plateau even though the Italians initially outnumbered them three to one.

The front quickly became another example of entrenched warfare, though, with the Austrians occupying the high ground. Five Battles of the Isonzo on the Italian border with Slovenia (then part of the Austro-Hungarian Empire) were fought with heavy casualties, between June 1915 and March 1916. All ended in stalemate. An Austro-Hungarian offensive also failed. This was followed by another five Battles of the Isonzo, all inconclusive. For the eleventh Battle of the Isonzo the Austro-Hungarians were supported by soldiers from the German army. On 24th October 1917 the Austrians and Germans launched the Battle of Caporetto, using gas shells as part of a huge artillery barrage. At the end of the first day, the Italians had retreated 12 miles to the Tagliamento River and were eventually pushed back to defensive lines near Venice on the Piave River.

On the 3rd and 4th November 1917 French and British troops landed in Italy to assist the Italian army. Private Reginald WEAVIL was amongst them. He was killed in action on 11th December in the Treviso Region.

The Sinai and Palestine Campaigns and the Suez Canal
Although nominally an autonomous province of the Ottoman Empire, Egypt had been occupied by the British since the Anglo-Egyptian War of 1882. This occupation meant that the British were able to defend the Suez Canal – the critical shipping link with much of the British Empire.

Knowing its strategic importance, in January 1915 a German-led Ottoman force invaded the Sinai Peninsula in an unsuccessful attack on the Canal. After the Gallipoli Campaign, ANZAC veterans were formed into the Egyptian Expeditionary Force and in 1916 began to take back control of Sinai. When the fighting stalled during 1917, reinforcements were sent from Europe.

It was on board SS *Transylvania* that some of these reinforcements were travelling when it was torpedoed off the Italian coast. Private Francis WATSON was amongst those who didn't survive.

In 1917 Bishop's Waltham lost 20 of its servicemen – the highest in any year of the war.

1918

The Western Front

Early in the war, in an attempt to mount a blockade on Britain, Germany had declared that all ships trading with Britain, including those of neutral countries such as the United States, would be targets for their submarines and would be sunk without warning. After the sinking of the RMS *Lusitania* by a German U-boat on 7th May 1915, war between the US and Germany was only averted when Germany vowed to cease this policy of unrestricted submarine warfare. On 17th January 1917 Germany rescinded this promise and again started sinking US merchant shipping. For this and other reasons the United States of America declared war on Germany on 6th April 1917.

It was immediately apparent to the German Supreme Command that it was just a matter of time before significant American forces were ready to join the fighting on the Western Front. In terms of timing they were fortunate that after the October Revolution of 1917, Russia had indicated that it would withdraw from the war and sue for peace. This released 50 German divisions which could be moved rapidly, by train, to the Western Front.

So, in the spring and summer of 1918 Germany committed thousands of troops, tons of equipment and hundreds of guns to a series of large-scale surprise offensives against the existing Allied lines, in an attempt to break the deadlock. After initial successes and some significant ground gained, the German offensives ran into difficulties because of stubborn resistance and their own over-stretched supply lines.

As part of their initial success, by 29th March 1918 the Germans had captured several key Allied-held towns on the Somme battlefield: Péronne, Ham, Noyon, Roye, Montdidier, Albert and Bapaume. It was on this day that Private Albert PURNELL went missing – presumed dead. Although the German advance had begun to stall, before it did so the Battle of Ancre was fought on 5th April. It may have been in this battle that Royal Marine Frank ANDREWS was killed. Royal Marine units had been part of the Royal Navy Division that had fought on the Western Front as foot soldiers since soon after the outbreak of war.

Meanwhile back in England, naval Gunner Harry ETHERIDGE was pensioned off on 1st April 1918 as physically unfit. It seems he was discharged from Haslar Hospital and later died from pulmonary tuberculosis at his mother's house on 19th July 1919. The last of the servicemen in this book to die.

On 9th April the Germans unleashed a new offensive – the Battle of Lys – designed to reach the French coast and cut off the British, French and Belgian troops in the Ypres Salient. Eight separate local battles took place between 9th and 29th April. It is probable that during one of these battles Corporal John APPS was killed in action on 20th April near Arras. He had been awarded the Military Medal for his bravery the year before.

A third German offensive – the Battle of the Aisne – was launched on 27th May and lasted until 2nd June. The bridges over the Aisne River were captured by the Germans and they had advanced approximately ten miles by the end of the first day. This was the greatest gain of ground in one day for either side since the end of the battles of 1914 in the "Race to the Sea". It was also the first time that American and German troops met in combat. Phase 4 (the Battle of Matz) and Phase 5 (the Second Battle of the Marne) of the German offensive took place in June and July-August respectively. They ended without any successful strategic conclusion and marked the beginning of the gradual retreat of the German forces during the second half of 1918.

A STORYLINE OF THE GREAT WAR

From July 1918 the Allies launched a series of offensives against a weakened German defensive line. This push by the Allied Armies on several parts of the Western Front succeeded in once again creating a war of movement and would become known as the 100 Day Offensive.

On 9th August, Captain John GUNNER died of wounds sustained at Kemmel, south of Ypres. Later in the month, on the 30th, Private Cecil DAVIS was killed in action in Flanders.

As the Allies broke through the Hindenburg Line, Private Esau RICHARDS died of wounds on 21st October most probably received during the Battle of the Selle (17th-26th October).

Sergeant Frank STUBBS had been in France since the beginning of 1918 and his battalion had also been part of the same offensive. Sadly, having survived the war he died on 14th November, three days after the Armistice, from influenza – very probably the 'Spanish Flu'. This was an unusually deadly influenza pandemic that lasted from 1918 to 1920, infected 500 million people around the world and resulted in the deaths of 50 to 100 million people (three to five percent of the world's population).

The Navy
On 16th September 1918 Petty Officer William COPP was serving on HMS *Glatton*. Whilst moored in Dover harbour, the vessel suffered an internal explosion and fire so severe that in a desperate move the Port Commodore, Vice Admiral Sir Roger Keyes, ordered it sunk before the fire spread to other ships. Three torpedoes from two different ships eventually succeeded in sinking the *Glatton*, thus putting out the fire. William Copp was one of the 79 men killed in the initial explosion or subsequent fire.

In the Skies
The Royal Flying Corps (RFC) was formed in 1912 with a military (army) wing and a naval wing (later hived off as the Royal Naval Air Service). On its

formation the RFC had just four squadrons – a balloon squadron and three 'heavier-than-air' squadrons, flying aircraft. The following year two more aircraft squadrons were added. By the end of March 1918, the RFC had expanded dramatically to comprise some 150 squadrons.

Initially used for artillery spotting and photographic reconnaissance, the RFC started tactical bombing in 1915 and increasingly became active participants rather than simply observers of what was happening on the ground. Aerial combat between aircraft led to a technological race to increase speed, manoeuvrability and firepower – there was a period in early 1917 when German planes held air superiority across most of the Western Front. As the war neared its end, the RFC was using bombs and machine gun fire to strafe and attack enemy trenches and positions, and the first long-range bombing missions against German communications and industry began.

Pilots flew throughout the Great War without parachutes because the self-pull ripcord necessary to deploy a parachute wasn't invented until 1919. Their planes were exposed to fire from the ground as well as the air. Casualties were high – for example, in support of the Battle of Arras in April 1917, the RFC deployed 25 squadrons, totalling 365 aircraft. The squadrons lost 245 aircraft with 211 aircrew killed or missing, and 108 taken as prisoners of war. A typically heavy toll.

Lieutenant Howard HEWETT had transferred from the East Kent Regiment to join 13 Squadron of the Royal Flying Corps after it moved to France in 1915. In October 1918 the squadron was based at Carnières, some four to fives miles east of Cambrai, and he died of his wounds on 27th October. It is possible that these had been inflicted flying during the Second Battle of Cambrai (8-10th October 1918) or more likely the follow-up Battle of the Selle (17-26th October).

Mesopotamia
As has already been said, casualties from diseases such as cholera, typhoid

and malaria were very high in the Mesopotamian campaign. On 17th November 1918 it claimed another victim, Private Theophilus BATT, who died just 17 days after the Armistice of Mudros. This Armistice, concluded on 30th October 1918, ended the hostilities in the Middle Eastern theatre between the Ottoman Empire and the Allies.

On 8th November 1918, Sapper George RICHARDS died in Gibraltar from unknown causes. It is possible he was wounded and being repatriated to Britain from the Middle East or one of the other Mediterranean fronts (such as Italy or Salonika) and died on the way.

In 1918 Bishop's Waltham lost 11 of its servicemen and, as recorded above, one more would die during 1919.

It is hoped that this narrative provides a sense of place, time and circumstance in which the men from Bishop's Waltham died.

Wounded soldiers and their nurses celebrate Armistice Day outside Northbrook House on 11th November 1918

In a Soldiers' Hospital: Pluck

Crippled for life at seventeen,
His great eyes seem to question why:
With both legs smashed it might have been
Better in that grim trench to die
Than drag maimed years out helplessly.

A child – so wasted and so white,
He told a lie to get his way,
To march, a man with men, and fight
While other boys are still at play.
A gallant lie your heart will say.

Eva Dobell

APPENDIX 1: WHERE THEY LIVED

Listed below is what we know, mainly from the censuses, about where, in the Bishop's Waltham area, the men named in this book lived before going to war.

NAME	PLACE(S) OF RESIDENCE
ANDREWS, Frank	1901 – living with his parents at Franklin Farmhouse, Corhampton. By 1911 he had left home. 1914 – married and set up home at **4 Victoria Buildings** (still exists).
ANDREWS, Frederick Charles	1901 – living with his parents at Franklin Farmhouse, Corhampton. 1911 – aged 30, living with his parents at **The Avenue, Newtown** (exact address unknown).
ANDREWS, Thomas Edwin	1901 – living with his parents at Franklin Farmhouse, Corhampton. 1911 – aged 16, living with his parents at **The Avenue, Newtown** (exact address unknown). By 1915, parents living in **Beeches Hill**.
APPS, John Henry	Family were living at Northbrook (exact address unknown) in 1891 and 1901, although he had left by then.
BAILEY, Ralph Ernest	1911 – aged 16, living with parents & siblings at **Green Lane Farm** (still exists), **Swanmore Road** (now Hoe Road).
BARFOOT, Edwin Albert	1901 – living with parents at **2 Claylands Cottages** (now demolished). 1911 – parents were living at **8 Victoria Road** (still exists) but Edwin had joined the Royal Marines.
BATT, Theophilus	In 1911 he was living at **1 Park Road** (still exists) with his wife and daughter; he was listed as "a baker and confectioner".
BELL, Charles Albert	1901 – aged 14, living with mother and siblings in **Bank Street** (exact address unknown). 1911 – mother still there, but Charles had left to join the Navy.

BEST, Ambrose Bert	1911 – aged 31, living with parents & two brothers at **1 Claylands Cottages** (now demolished).
BRUCE, Donald	Parents moved to Bishop's Waltham before 1909. 1911 – father was living alone in Dean.
CASEY, George Gordon	1910 – at time of enlisting, he was a schoolteacher living in Bishop's Waltham (exact address unknown).
CONDUCT, Leonard Albert	1911 – aged 20, living with parents at **15 Victoria Buildings** (now demolished), and working at the Brick & Tile Works.
CONDUCT, William Edward	1911 – living with parents at **15 Victoria Buildings** (now demolished), and working at the Brick & Tile Works.
COOK, Frederick Alexander	1901 - living with parents at **11 Claylands Cottages** (now demolished). 1911 – aged 14, living with parents at 1 Pondside Terrace (still exists).
COPP, William Jacob	His family moved to **The Hangers** (exact address unknown) by 1911 but he had left home. At his death in 1918 his mother was living at **4 Garfield Road** (still exists).
COTTLE, George James	1901 – parents lived in Shedfield but George had left area. Mother then died. 1915 – father and stepmother had moved to **Garfield Road** (exact address unknown).
CUTLER, William John	1901 – aged 3, living with parents in **Free Street** (exact address unknown); father was a blacksmith. 1911 – living in **Bank Street** (exact address unknown).
DAVIS, Cecil	Born 1891 in **Fry's Lane, Meonstoke**. In 1911 he was working at The Kennels, Droxford.
EMMETT, Albert Henry	1901 – living with parents in **Sciviers Lane, Upham**. 1911 – working as a groom at Marwell Hall.
EMMETT, Alfred Henry	Born in Bishop's Waltham in 1894. 1911 – living in **Hedge End**.

APPENDIX 1: WHERE THEY LIVED

EPPS, Louis	1901 – aged 7, living with parents in Free Street (exact address unknown). 1911 – parents lived at **Albion Cottage, Free Street** (still exists) but Louis had moved to London by then.
ETHERIDGE, Harry	1891 – living with his mother in **Basingwell Street** (exact address unknown). 1901 – family living in **Houchin Street**. 1911 – he was on board HMS *Prince George*.
FURSEY, William Arthur	1911 – living with parents in **Lower Lane** (exact address unknown).
GARSIDE, William Henry	Family lived in Swanmore in 1911.
GIBSON, Herbert	Born in Swanmore. On his death in 1914, his widow was living in **Bank Street**.
GIBSON, Neil Stewart	At his death in 1917, his place of residence was Upham.
GIFFARD-BRINE, Robin George Bruce	Born in 1899 to parents living in **Highfield, Winchester Road** (now demolished). No information from 1901 & 1911 censuses.
GORE, Edward Patrick	1911 – living with parents at The Fir Tree Inn, Upham.
GUNNER, Benjamin George	Born at **Ridgemede House** (now a care home). Went to Sandhurst in 1911.
GUNNER, Edward Geoffrey	Born at **Ridgemede House**. Left home to train as a naval officer.
GUNNER, John Hugh	Born at **Ridgemede House**. Married in 1909; in 1911 was living in Botley.
HAMMOND, Charlie	1901 and 1911 – living with parents in **Free Street** (exact address unknown).
HAMMOND, Herbert	1891 and 1901 – living with his parents in Waltham Chase (exact address unknown). 1911 – serving on HMS *Illustrious*.

HARVELL, Frederick William	1901 – living with parents at **Primrose Terrace, Beeches Hill** (exact address unknown). 1911 – father had died, Frederick had left home and mother was living in **Bank Street**.
HEWETT, Howard Dudley	1901 – aged 4, living in **Portland Square** (where Lower Lane car park is now). During the war he corresponded with his father who was living at **Waiwera, Winchester Road** (now demolished).
HEWETT, William John	1911 – aged 34, he was living with his wife and 3 children in **Coppice Hill** (exact address unknown). At his death his widow was living at **Strathavon, Crown Hill** (still exists).
HIGGINS, Francis	1901 – living with parents at **3 Vernon Hill Cottages** (still exists). 1911 – family was living in **Basingwell Street** (exact address unknown); Francis had gone to live in Fontley.
KING, Andrew Buchanan	1912 – married the daughter of Rev. H.E. Sharpe (Rector of Bishop's Waltham from 1913-1931).
LACEY, Henry Percy Walter	1911 – aged 17, living with his mother and stepfather in **St Peter's Street** (exact address unknown).
LEE, Ernest Edward	1891 – visitor at the home of Paul Desa (photographer) in **School Hill** (exact address unknown). 1901 & 1911 – boarding with the Desas in **Brook Street** (exact address unknown). 1911 Kelly's Directory – Desa was photographer and shopkeeper in **Red Lion St** (exact address unknown).
LOVELL, George	1901 – living with parents at **3 Primrose Terrace**, Beeches Hill (still exists). 1911 – parents lived at **2 Margaret Cottages, Beeches Hill** (still exists), but George had left to join the RMA.
MATTHEWS, William	1911 – living with parents at Longwood Dean. 1916 – after his death, William's pension was sent to his widow at two addresses (one was **4 Primrose Cottages, Beeches Hill**, which still exists).

APPENDIX 1: WHERE THEY LIVED

MAY, William Edgar	1901 – aged 6, living with parents at **Strete End** (exact address unknown). 1911 – living with parents in **Houchin Street** (exact address unknown).
MEARS, Walter	1891 and 1901 – living with parents at **Myrtle Cottage, Winchester Road**. 1911 – parents lived in Waltham Chase (exact address unknown) but Walter had joined the RMA. Walter married in 1913 and moved into Valetta Cottage, Waltham Chase.
NEWLAND, George William	1911 – living and working as a farmer in Dean (exact address unknown).
PAICE, Archibald Stanley	1891 – living with parents at **Brewery House** (now demolished). 1901 – living with parents at The Elms, Station Road (now demolished). 1911 - parents still at The Elms; Archibald was living in Reading.
PRICE, Jack Benjamin	1901 – Alton. 1911 – Jubilee Tavern (now The Hampshire Bowman PH), Dundridge.
PRICE, Walter	Had been living in Dundridge at the Jubilee Tavern (now The Hampshire Bowman PH).
PURNELL, Albert Edward	1911 – living with his family at **11 Claylands Cottages** (now demolished).
RICHARDS, Esau	1911 – his family were living in the **High Street** (exact address unknown) where his father Arthur had a jewellery shop.
RICHARDS, George Solomon	1911 – the family were living in **Winchester Road** (exact address unknown) but he had left by then.
RICHARDS, William Henry	1901 and 1911 – living with parents in **Winchester Road** (exact address unknown).
SIMS, Arthur Follett	1891 – living with parents in **The School House** (adjoining school at corner of Victoria Road and Albert Road). By 1901 he had joined Navy. Father still at The School House when Arthur died.
SIMS, Oswald Follett	1901 and 1911 – living with parents at **The School House**.

SMITH, Charles Henry	1901 – aged 8 living with parents at Lower Farm Cottage, Exton. 1911 – a farm labourer boarding in **Curdridge Lane** (exact address unknown), Bishop's Waltham.
STEELE, William Charles	1911 – a visitor at the home of George Tilbury, **Bank Street** (exact address unknown). 1913 – he married Tilbury's daughter.
STUBBS, Frank Austin	1911 – was listed as "a clerk to auctioneer" and living with his parents at **Wolversdene** (still exists) in **Hoe Road**.
WATSON, Francis	1909 – married Blanche Emily New of Bishop's Waltham. 1911 – living at **Gilberts Knapp, Beeches Hill** (Blanche's father's house), which still exists.
WEAVIL, Reginald Frank	1901 – living with parents at Ladysmith Terrace (still exists). 1911 – living with parents at **Albany Terrace, Newtown**.
WEEKS, Edwin	1911 – living with parents at Beauworth. When awarded his medals, his mother was living in **Basingwell Street** (exact address unknown).
WEEKS, Wilfred Joseph	During the War his mother was living in **Basingwell Street** (exact address unknown).

APPENDIX 1: WHERE THEY LIVED

Warbride

This is the bitterest wrong the world wide,
That young men on the battlefield should rot,
And I be widowed who was scarce a bride,
While prattling old men sit at ease and plot.

Nina Murdoch

APPENDIX 2: CEMETERIES AND MEMORIALS OF THE GREAT WAR

This Appendix features some of the main cemeteries and memorials on the Western Front and beyond, where men from Bishop's Waltham are buried or commemorated.

The Commonwealth War Graves Commission (CWGC) was formed in 1917 (as the Imperial War Graves Commission) and had an extraordinary role. It was given the massive task of providing cemeteries and memorials to bury and commemorate the 1.1 million servicemen of the Empire who died in the Great War. By 1921 the Commission had responsibility for 2,400 cemeteries, for which more than half a million headstones, of Portland stone and of uniform shape and size, were made. For the tens of thousands of servicemen who were missing and had no known grave, impressive memorials were constructed.

Cemeteries

On a ridge near Ypres in Belgium is Tyne Cot Cemetery. It is the Commonwealth's largest cemetery in the world, containing around 12,000 graves together with memorial panels with around 35,000 names of those who died in the battlefields around Ypres and have no known grave. In particular many thousands died in the Battle of Passchendaele (also known as the Third Battle of Ypres) in the fields overlooked by this vast cemetery. On the memorial at Tyne Cot are the names of two men from Bishop's Waltham: George William NEWLAND and Wilfred Joseph WEEKS.

There are many cemeteries beyond the Western Front. Of particular interest are those on the hills overlooking the Dardanelles Strait, where the calamitous campaign at Gallipoli was fought in 1915. Allied forces met ferocious opposition from Turkish troops. Tens of thousands of ANZAC troops (from Australia and New Zealand) were killed, and more than 4,900 are buried or commemorated at the Lone Pine Cemetery, including Ralph Ernest BAILEY (who had been buried at sea).

APPENDIX 2: CEMETERIES AND MEMORIALS OF THE GREAT WAR

© Jurga Van Steenbergen https://fullsuitcase.com
Tyne Cot cemetery near Ypres

Lone Pine Cemetery, Gallipoli

WE WILL REMEMBER THEM

Many of the servicemen commemorated in this book died in France or Belgium and are buried in the many cemeteries, looked after by the CWGC, that dot the landscape in this region. There are also similarly well-kept cemeteries wherever British or Commonwealth soldiers fought and died – for instance in Iraq, Macedonia and Italy. This gravestone for Private Francis HIGGINS, in the Ypres Town Cemetery Extension, is included below to represent the many.

APPENDIX 2: CEMETERIES AND MEMORIALS OF THE GREAT WAR

Memorials

Also on the Gallipoli peninsula is the imposing Helles Memorial, 100 ft tall, standing on high ground above Cape Helles and visible to all ships entering the Dardanelles. It lists the names of nearly 21,000 men who died during the Gallipoli campaign but have no known grave. Included on this monument are the names of Leonard Albert CONDUCT and William Charles STEELE.

The Helles Memorial

The founder of modern Turkey, Mustafa Kemal Atatürk, first made his name as the regimental commander who fought against the Commonwealth forces at ANZAC Cove. In 1934, as President of Turkey, he had a memorial erected near the ANZAC Cove cemetery to recognise the sacrifice of both sides. It is a testament to reconciliation.

WE WILL REMEMBER THEM

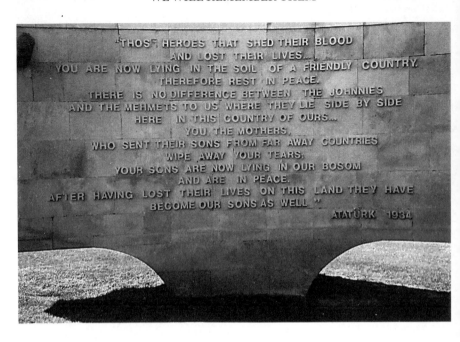

It reads:
"THOSE HEROES THAT SHED THEIR BLOOD
AND LOST THEIR LIVES…
YOU ARE NOW LYING IN THE SOIL OF A FRIENDLY COUNTRY
THEREFORE REST IN PEACE.
THERE IS NO DIFFERENCE BETWEEN THE JOHNNIES
AND THE MEHMETS TO US WHERE THEY LIE SIDE BY SIDE
HERE IN THIS COUNTRY OF OURS…
YOU, THE MOTHERS,
WHO SENT THEIR SONS FROM FARAWAY COUNTRIES
WIPE AWAY YOUR TEARS;
YOUR SONS ARE NOW LYING IN OUR BOSOM
AND ARE IN PEACE.
AFTER HAVING LOST THEIR LIVES ON THIS LAND THEY HAVE
BECOME OUR SONS AS WELL"

ATATÜRK 1934

APPENDIX 2: CEMETERIES AND MEMORIALS OF THE GREAT WAR

The memorial is curved so that the words, when read out loud, echo back to the reader.

On the Western Front

Fierce fighting took place in the Ypres Salient during much of the War. To commemorate the missing, the impressive Menin Gate Memorial in Ypres was constructed, on which are the names of more than 54,000 officers and men. Three men from Bishop's Waltham are included: Alfred Harry EMMETT, William MATTHEWS and Walter PRICE.

The Menin Gate was chosen because hundreds of thousands of Allied soldiers had passed through it on the way to the battlefields. The memorial, designed by the eminent architect Sir Reginald Blomfield, is neither triumphal nor celebratory. Every night at 8pm the Last Post is sounded, in a very moving ceremony.

© Jurga Van Steenbergen https://fullsuitcase.com

Menin Gate, Ypres

The battle of the Somme, which lasted from July to November 1916, is etched into the collective memory of the British as probably the most horrific and tragic battle in our history. On the first day alone nearly 60,000 were killed or wounded. As a memorial to the missing of the Somme, the massive edifice at Thiepval was built, the largest Commonwealth War Graves Commission memorial in the world. Designed by the great Edwardian architect Sir Edwin Lutyens, and built of brick and stone with huge square pillars and arches, the Thiepval memorial is visible for miles around. On the memorial's panels are the names of more than 72,000 officers and men who died on the Somme but have no known grave. Included are the names of three men from Bishop's Waltham, all of whom were serving in the Hampshire Regiment: William Edward CONDUCT, Louis EPPS and Charlie HAMMOND.

Thiepval Memorial to the Missing of the Somme in Picardy

APPENDIX 2: CEMETERIES AND MEMORIALS OF THE GREAT WAR

Portsmouth Naval Memorial
The CWGC is also responsible for memorials to sailors, and the most significant one for us in Bishop's Waltham is the monumental Portsmouth Naval Memorial on the seafront at Southsea, designed by the versatile Scottish architect Sir Robert Lorimer. On this memorial are commemorated around 10,000 sailors of the Great War (and about 15,000 of WWII). Local men include Charles Albert BELL, Patrick GORE, Edward Geoffrey GUNNER, and Herbert HAMMOND.

The following five men lost their lives on 31st May 1916 during the Battle of Jutland: Frederick Charles ANDREWS, Edwin Albert BARFOOT, Robin George GIFFARD-BRINE, George LOVELL, and Walter MEARS. Their names are to be found there too.

Portsmouth Naval Memorial

WE WILL REMEMBER THEM

The entry for Patrick Gore, Boy Telegraphist, on the Portsmouth Naval Memorial – the youngest serviceman from Bishop's Waltham to die, aged just 16

One only has to visit any one of these many cemeteries and memorials to feel the scale of the loss.

Bishop's Waltham Church and Churchyard

The CWGC is also responsible for some graves in the churchyards of cities, towns and villages around the country. There are two Commonwealth War Graves in St Peter's Churchyard that relate to The Great War: Thomas Edwin ANDREWS, one of the three Andrews brothers who died during the War; and George James COTTLE, who died of lung disease in February 1917. Also buried in the churchyard, but in a private grave, is Harry ETHERIDGE (see photo on page 56), who died of tuberculosis on 19th July 1919.

APPENDIX 2: CEMETERIES AND MEMORIALS OF THE GREAT WAR

The CWGC gravestone of Thomas Edwin Andrews in St Peter's Churchyard

Photo by Frank Grant

Private war grave of George James Cottle also in St Peter's Churchyard

WE WILL REMEMBER THEM

The memorial to Midshipman Robin 'Chips' Giffard-Brine, the second youngest to die at age 17, in St Peter's Church

Memorial plaque to John Hugh Gunner in St Peter's Church

APPENDIX 2: CEMETERIES AND MEMORIALS OF THE GREAT WAR

In Flanders Fields

In Flanders fields the poppies blow
Between the crosses, row on row,
That mark our place; and in the sky
The larks, still bravely singing, fly
Scarce heard amid the guns below.

We are the Dead. Short days ago
We lived, felt dawn, saw sunset glow,
Loved and were loved, and now we lie
In Flanders fields.
Take up our quarrel with the foe:
To you from failing hands we throw
The torch; be yours to hold it high.
If ye break faith with us who die
We shall not sleep, though poppies grow
In Flanders fields.

John McMrae

APPENDIX 3: MEDALS AND BADGES

The 1914 Star

The 1914 Star is a bronze medal, also called The Mons Star. Only about 378,000 were issued, mostly to members of the British and Indian Expeditionary Force who fought in France between the day after Britain's declaration of war on Germany (5th August 1914) and the end of the First Battle of Ypres (midnight 22nd November 1914). The majority of recipients were officers and men of the pre-war British army, specifically the British Expeditionary Force, many also known as the Old Contemptibles, who landed in France soon after the outbreak of the War and who took part in the Retreat from Mons, hence the medal's nickname, "Mons Star". Some Royal Navy personnel received the medal as did some Canadians and women, who served as nurses, with the BEF. A thousand medals were also awarded to members of the Royal Flying Corps who served in the same period.

It is a four-pointed star with a crown on the uppermost point. It has two swords positioned to make four additional points, overlaid with a wreath of oak leaves. At the bottom is the Royal Cypher of George V and there is an S-shaped scroll inscribed AUG 1914 NOV across the centre. The ribbon has the red, white and blue colours of the flag of the United Kingdom in shaded and watered bands. The Bishop's Waltham servicemen who were awarded this medal were Ambrose BEST, Harry ETHERIDGE, Herbert GIBSON, William HEWETT, Andrew KING, William MATTHEWS and Walter PRICE.

APPENDIX 3: MEDALS AND BADGES

The 1914-15 Star

The 1914–15 Star was instituted in December 1918. It was awarded to officers and men of the British and Imperial forces who served against the Central European Powers in any theatre of the Great War between 5th August 1914 and 31st December 1915, provided they had not already received the 1914 Star. The period of eligibility was prior to the Military Service Act 1916, which introduced conscription in Britain. Some 2,400,000 were issued.

In form it is identical to the 1914 Star except that the central scroll is inscribed 1914-1915. Those servicemen entitled to the 1914-15 Star were: Leonard CONDUCT, Frederick COOK, Alfred EMMETT, William GARSIDE, Robin GIFFARD-BRINE, Herbert HAMMOND, Ernest LEE, William MAY, George NEWLAND, George RICHARDS, William RICHARDS and Edwin WEEKS.

The British War Medal

The British War Medal was instituted on 26th July 1919 as an award to those who had rendered service between the start of the war on 5th August 1914 and the armistice of 11th November 1918. As a historical footnote, eligibility was subsequently extended to cover service over 1919 and 1920 in mine-clearing at sea. It was also extended to those who participated in operations in North and South Russia, the eastern Baltic region, Siberia, the Black Sea and the Caspian Sea, during the allied intervention in the Russian Civil War. Approximately 6,400,000 servicemen from Britain and the Empire received this award. It is a silver medal with the head of George V and its ribbon is watered silk with blue edges with a black and then white stripe down each side and a central band of orange.

The Allied Victory Medal

In March 1919 a joint committee set up by the Allies proposed that each Allied nation should design a Victory Medal to award to their own nationals. The common features to all would be a winged figure of Victory and the colour of the ribbon. Fifteen different countries designed and awarded their own medal.

Britain's Victory Medal was issued to all those who received the 1914 Star or the 1914–15 Star, and to most of those who were awarded the British War Medal. As with the British War Medal, it was also awarded for mine clearance in the North Sea until 30th November 1919 and for participation in the Allied intervention in the Russian Civil War up to 1st July 1920. About 5,700,000 of these medals were issued.

Made of bronze with a lacquer finish, it features the winged, full-length, full-front, figure of 'Victory' with her left arm extended and holding a palm branch in her right hand, similar to the statue surmounting the Queen Victoria Memorial, in front of Buckingham Palace in London. On the other side of the medal are the words "THE GREAT WAR FOR CIVILISATION 1914-1919".

Sets of these medals had nicknames – nobody seems to know how they arose. A Star plus a War and a Victory medal were called "Pip, Squeak and Wilfred", apparently after animal cartoon characters in a *Daily Mirror* cartoon (a dog, a penguin and a long-eared rabbit), while the War and Victory medals became known as "Mutt and Jeff", who were characters from the world's first ever comic strip. These were originally published in the *San Francisco Chronicle* but later became widely syndicated to other newspapers worldwide.

APPENDIX 3: MEDALS AND BADGES

The Silver War Badge

This award was not a military medal. It was created in 1916, and was initially issued to officers and men who were honourably discharged from the Forces due to injury or illness caused by their war service. In early 1918 eligibility was extended to include civilians serving with the Royal Army Medical Corps, female nurses, staff and aid workers. The primary reason for issue was to prevent such people from being wrongly presented with a "White Feather" by women wishing to humiliate apparently able men not in uniform, which they had done in the early part of the war to boost the numbers who volunteered to join the Forces.

Introduced in 1916, the badge was a large sterling silver lapel badge and was intended to be worn on the right breast on civilian clothes. The decoration was introduced as an award of the "King's silver" for having received wounds or been taken ill during loyal war service to the Crown. Approximately 1,150,000 badges were issued (all of which had to be claimed and then approved), which indicates the number of war wounded who were discharged from service during the Great War. Harry ETHERIDGE, from Bishop's Waltham, was granted a Silver War Badge in March 1918 after his discharge.

Gallantry Medals

In addition to the above awards, of course, there were the medals given in response to personal acts of courage.

The Military Medal

The Military Medal was established in 1916, with retrospective application to 1914, and was awarded to other ranks, including non-commissioned officers (sergeants and corporals) and warrant officers (in other words, soldiers below commissioned officer rank) for "acts of gallantry and devotion to duty under fire". Although designed for British and Imperial armed forces, it was also awarded to other services – some French soldiers who fought on the Somme in 1916 were awarded the medal.

It ranked below the Distinguished Conduct Medal, which was also awarded to other ranks. During the Great War around five times more Military Medals were awarded than Distinguished Conduct Medals. However, some 115,000 awards of the Military Medal were made for acts of gallantry or devotion to duty during the Great War.

It is a silver medal and for the Great War it bore the effigy of George V. The other side of the medal states, quite simply, "FOR BRAVERY IN THE FIELD". The ribbon is dark blue with five equal centre stripes that are white, red, white, red, and white. Private John APPS, from Bishop's Waltham, was awarded the Military Medal in 1917.

APPENDIX 3: MEDALS AND BADGES

The Military Cross
The award was created at the end of 1914 for commissioned officers with the rank of captain or lieutenant as well as for warrant officers. It was awarded in recognition of "an act or acts of exemplary gallantry during active operations against the enemy on land". It is in the form of an ornamental silver cross with straight arms terminating in broad finials, suspended from a plain suspension bar. It is decorated with four imperial crowns, with the Royal Cypher in the centre. The ribbon has three equal vertical moiré stripes of white, purple, and white. Around 40,000 Military Crosses were awarded during the Great War. Captain Benjamin GUNNER received the Military Cross in June 1915.

For the Fallen

They shall not grow old as we that are left grow old,
Age shall not weary them, nor the years condemn.
At the going down of the sun and in the morning
We will remember them.

Laurence Binyon